D0327977

EXPERT RULES

100 (and More) Points
You Need to Know About
Expert Witnesses

EXPERT RULES

100 (and More) Points
You Need to Know About
Expert Witnesses

Second Edition

David M. Malone
Paul J. Zwier

National Institute for Trial Advocacy

© 1999, 2001 by the National Institute for Trial Advocacy
Printed in the United States of America. All rights reserved.

These materials, or any parts or portions thereof, may not be
reproduced in any form, written or mechanical, or be
programmed into any electronic storage or retrieval system
without the express written permission of the National
Institute for Trial Advocacy.

Copies of these materials are available from the National
Institute for Trial Advocacy. Please direct inquiries to:

National Institute for Trial Advocacy
Notre Dame Law School
Notre Dame, IN 46556-6500
(800) 225-6482
Fax: (219) 271-8375
Web site: www.nita.org
E-mail: nita.1@nd.edu

Malone, David M. and Paul J. Zwier, *Expert Rules: 100 (and
More) Points You Need to Know About Expert Witnesses, Second
Edition* (NITA, 2001).

ISBN 1-55681-721-5

Table of Contents

Introduction

Socrates asked the Delphic Oracle, "Who is the wisest man in the world?" The Oracle replied, "Socrates." Rubbing his toe in the dust and looking abashedly downward, Jimmy Stewart-like, Socrates said, "That can't be true. There's so much that I know I don't know." "Exactly," answered the Oracle. From this, Socrates extracted the lesson that he taught his students: "The man who does not know, and does not know that he does not know, is a fool."

In our introduction to the Revised First Edition, we focused with some excitement on the changes imposed on expert practice by the *Daubert* and *Kumho Tire* cases. The challenge to trial attorneys was to find ways of testing the reliability of experts' methodologies, and then to present the weaknesses in the methodologies to judges who are not themselves experts in the discipline under scrutiny. Many questions about the admissibility of expert testimony will be resolved through application of no more than the four topics suggested by the Supreme Court for assessing reliability: publication in peer-reviewed journals; analysis of the error rate; general acceptance in the relevant scientific community; and testability, replicability, and falsifiability. Indeed, organized examination of two or three of these characteristics of the proffered "science" will result in more disciplined evaluation of the experts' offering than was generally seen before *Daubert-Kumho*. Indeed, even before the *Daubert* trilogy (here including *General Electric v. Joiner*, on the standard of review), there were large budget cases, docketed in multiple forums, that raised these questions, but now these questions are being asked in more routine cases, of experts whose fields had previously been unchallenged. (Indeed, the December, 2000 amendments to Federal Rules of Evidence 701–703 incorporate the *Daubert* changes. The amended rules are appended on page 123. Rule 701 clarifies that non-expert opinions are limited to those not based on "scientific, technical, or other specialized knowledge." Rule 702 now incorporates the *Daubert* standard of reliable methodology correctly applied. And Rule 703 settles the dispute over whether inadmissible bases may be disclosed to the jury by the proponent — ordinarily they may not.)

Our increased sophistication leads us now to put these expert questions in a broader context. We ask not only, "What is the evidence that leads us to believe that this methodology is sufficiently reliable?" but also, "How does the expert know that he knows something?" and "How do we know that he knows?" No lie detector test is adequate here; it would eliminate the lying experts (who we hope would be eliminated by traditional approaches on deposition and cross-examination), but it would not eliminate the expert who in good faith believes that she is correct and knowledgeable, when in fact she is not. Instead, she is the person who does not know, but does not know that she does not know.

In *G.E. v. Joiner*, the Supreme Court directed trial courts to avoid reliance on the *ipse dixit* of the expert; just because the expert witness says it is so — the methodology is reliable, the use is appropriate, the error rate is acceptable — that does not make it so, either. Similarly, the fact that other experts in the field have been saying "it" in court for a long time does not make it so, either. Microeconomists have long counseled that reduced concentration in industries will result in increased innovation, greater product variety and lower prices; yet we are still nervous about the remedy proposed in the Microsoft antitrust litigation — we would prefer something more than theory before we restructure what might well be the engine of the country's recent economic success.[1]

All of this time spent in "hard thinking" should lead us to improved expert selection and presentation. When we thought that anyone with a briefcase who came from out of town would be accepted as an expert, we could shop for the one whose opinion was most acceptable (or needed the least burnishing). Now that we know that experts will be routinely examined to determine the strength and reliability of their foundations, we must select our experts more carefully, and present them more rationally. We, as trial lawyers, must find ways to demonstrate that the expert "knows," and that she "knows that she knows."

---

1. It is interesting to think about the fact that, of the four criteria mentioned in *Daubert*, only "peer-reviewed publication" is available to support most microeconomic testimony, especially of the structural (number of firms in an industry) variety. There is no calculated error rate for dismantling major industries: the Standard Oil trust-busting may have instilled competition, but maybe only at the retail level — more food products made available at stations, four stations at every intersection. Given the dominance of world oil exports by OPEC, we really have no competitive market to evaluate. The breakup of AT&T may have produced some increased competition in long-distance service, but it is very difficult to estimate what would have happened if AT&T had remained as it was to confront the technological revolution we have seen since 1976, when the first Apple computer was born. This is not to argue that AT&T should not have been

The "delight and charm" that Degas mentions in his letter (quoted in the introduction to the first edition) has exploded into starbursts of light and dark matter, as we struggle to shoulder our small portion of the burden of distinguishing human knowledge from human ignorance.

David M. Malone

Paul J. Zwier

---

broken up; it merely illustrates that we have little experience with the restructuring of important industries, so it is somewhat circular (and dangerous) to present that minimal past experience as a justification for proposed restructuring of additional industries. So long as the Harvard school contests every proposal made by the Chicago school (and vice verse), it is difficult to conclude that there is general acceptance of any approach in the relevant (microeconomic) scientific community. And no aspects of testability for such restructuring — replicability or falsifiability — are reproducible in a laboratory or classroom setting. Some other indicia of reliability of the proposed methodology must be examined in order to determine whether we want the courts basing important decisions on this "science."

Expert Rules

Introduction to the First Edition

Even before the watershed opinions in *Daubert v. Merrill Dow Pharmaceuticals, Inc.*, 509 U.S. 579 (1993) and *Kumho Tire Co., Ltd. v. Carmichael*, 526 U.S. 137 (1999), experts confronted lawyers with some of the most interesting and challenging questions in trial preparation and presentation: *When can they be used? What can they rely on? What can be discovered? What can they be told? What can they tell us? How can they be challenged?* And, perhaps the most challenging question on experts: *How can the courts divide the "good science" from the bad?*

In *Daubert* and *Kumho*, the Supreme Court resolved some old questions but created many new ones — questions with which trial and appellate courts will continue to struggle. We now know, from *Kumho Tire*, that it is the proffer of expert *knowledge* in the courtroom — whether scientific, technical, or other specialized knowledge — which calls for the trial court to assess the reliability of such testimony as a gatekeeper, as described in *Daubert*. But those cases invited the courts, and practitioners, to propose criteria for gauging reliability on a case by case, expert by expert, basis. Thus, the *Daubert* standards of peer-reviewed publication, known or knowable error rate, acceptance in the relevant field, and testability or replicability, are recognized as inappropriate for some disciplines. Trial lawyers and trial courts must work together to find additional criteria which serve the purpose of separating wheat from chaff, gold from dross, and good science from junk science.

In *Daubert* and *Kumho Tire*, dealing with statistical epidemiology and mechanical engineering, respectively, the Court applied principles of reliability appropriate to those disciplines, perhaps based upon some *a priori* belief that the disciplines were reliable and therefore were the appropriate starting point for assessing the reliability of the methodologies employed in the particular cases. It seems unlikely, however, that principles from astrology will be accepted as providing guidance for assessing the reliability of an astrologer's testimony; acupuncture, chiropractic and creation science pose additional problems. *Kumho Tire* answered some questions left from *Daubert*; now we must resolve questions left by both.

There are many questions regarding experts in litigation which have answers, however, and it is the purpose of this book to provide some of those answers to the trial attorney who is looking for logical guidance as she prepares her case. The authors have tried to raise common issues and provide useful approaches; we have not tried to present the law in the form of controlling or leading cases which can be cited to a court. When an expert issue grows to the point at which briefing to the court is necessary, resources other than this book are clearly required; but when the trial lawyer merely needs some feel for how to approach an expert problem, or wants to review the structure of direct examination of an expert, or wants to avoid potentially fatal blunders in preparing an expert (and feeding him information pre-trial), then, we hope, this book will be a quick and useful aid.

Here is our recommendation on how to get the most out of this book: Read it once, all the way through (especially the rules of evidence and civil procedure we have included at the back), as soon as you have time; read pertinent parts as you begin dealing with your next expert or begin the next steps with a current expert; check the index for relevant portions when your opponent does something with her expert that you had not expected; and write to us, through the National Institute for Trial Advocacy, to point out additional questions and answers that we should include in the next edition, or to tell us about problems or successes you have encountered following our advice.

In a context unknown to us, the painter Edgar Degas once wrote: *"What a delightful thing is the conversation of specialists! One understands absolutely nothing and it's charming."* Degas captures the charm and delight that we feel in dealing with experts, in learning their fields, at being educated or challenged by them, and in challenging them in turn. He could not know, however, that we as trial attorneys cannot afford to understand "absolutely nothing." Therefore, take up the challenge, learn the rules, and enjoy the good fight.

David M. Malone

Paul J. Zwier

A. Finding an Expert

A.1. There is no requirement that experts be from the jurisdiction involved in the suit, or even from this country.

Foreign experts can testify in person or by deposition, although the costs of such a deposition, including travel by the opposing attorneys, may have to be borne by the sponsor of the expert. Note, however, that in medical malpractice cases, where an expert must be called by the plaintiff to testify to the standard of care, some jurisdictions set up a presumption favoring an expert from that state. For example, Virginia presumes that a medical expert who practices in the state qualifies; nevertheless, Virginia also requires that any expert be able to testify that he or she both knows the standard of medical practice in the locality **and** has had a clinical practice in the field within the last year. In addition, Virginia provides that, **"when appropriate,"** the standard of care might be set by the locality. Where the court so finds, it seems logical that the expert would have to know the standard of practice in that locality. To be safe it probably is easier for the plaintiff to look first for a practicing physician expert in the locality of the defendant's practice, in order to insure that the expert will know the standard of practice in that locality (especially if the court will choose to apply that locality's standard of practice). See, Va.Civ. Code 8.01-581.20. See also, Section A.5.

A.2. Look inside the client's organization for an expert, especially for a non-testifying expert.

The following areas are often sources of helpful expertise: product development departments (product liability, toxic torts, inadequate warnings, patent, antitrust), sales (antitrust, trademark), accounting (antitrust, contract, patent), marketing (advertising, antitrust), engineering (product liability, inadequate warnings, environmental, patent). [Warning: If these experts have already studied the product or business in dispute for non-litigation purposes, they may have documents that contain admissions that could be damaging to the case. If you select these witnesses, you may lead your opponent to the discovery of damaging evidence. Of course, such documents may be subject to discovery or disclosure anyhow.]

A.3. Look outside, especially for testifying experts, if it is important to avoid the apparent bias held by an employee-expert.

Look at local educational institutions, other cases in local courts, experts used by colleagues, national educational institutions, publications in the field, web sites of expert organizations, and expert directories or services. Look outside for a consulting expert if you are not sure you are getting all the facts from the client. The outside consulting expert will ask the right questions to lead you to get a more objective look at the case. Then you are better able to turn around and ask these same questions of the client.

A.4. The bias by the trier-of-fact for a local expert may be outweighed by the non-local expert's logic, interesting presentation, apparent honesty, relevant experience, or national reputation.

While the trier-of-fact may be interested in any well-presented, well-spoken expert, he is likely to be specially impressed at meeting a high-level expert from a famous institution. Thus, the prejudice against the outsider may be outweighed by deference to the world famous visitor. As is recommended, emphasize whatever differences exist between your expert and your opponents; make them into qualifications; present them on visual exhibits and talk about them in your jury speeches; with regard to your expert, make the judge and jury think that different is better. (See Rule A.10, below.)

A.5. Except in medical and legal malpractice cases, there is no requirement of familiarity by the expert with any local "standards of care."

(See Section A.2.) However, industry practices, jurisdictional building codes, and similar information are information of which the expert must be aware.

A.6. Substantial cases deserve substantial experts.

Harvard professors not only seem smart — they are smart. Furthermore, their superior experience and connections often permit them to accomplish the expert tasks more efficiently, so that their "doubled" hourly rates do not result in doubled total expert fees. Of course, there is some ambiguity in the word "substantial." If "substantial" means the amount of money in controversy, then the client will have less trouble with spending money to get it or protect it. Where the amount is in doubt (either because you need a damages expert or a causation expert to tell you whether there is a mass tort potential to this case), you might first want to hire a consulting expert, to help you explain to the client why you think the case is substantial.

A.7. When two experts are reasonably equally qualified, choose the expert with whom you

feel more comfortable working and spending time.

If you and the expert do not enjoy working together, then you will tend to avoid the frequent communication and long hours of preparation that are necessary to succeed. You can think of this as the "glass of beer" test: if you wouldn't enjoy sitting down and having a glass of beer with the expert, then you probably shouldn't hire her, if you have any choice at all. Expert work is hard enough without overlaying it with personality problems (even if it is your personality that is at fault).

A.8. Hands-on experts who have gained a substantial portion of their expertise through experience and training as opposed to "book-learning," have a persuasive advantage in cases involving *application* of principles, as opposed to *explanation* of principles.

For example, in a car crash case, an engineer who designs cars may be more credible than a professor of metallurgical engineering who can calculate tensile and compression strengths of steel alloys used in car frames.

A.9. Local experts, or experts who have gained a substantial portion of their expertise through experience or training, may be at a disadvantage

in cases where significant *Daubert* challenges are anticipated.

For example, in cases involving causation in theory or analysis of relatively new, complex, or unusual scientific evidence, a "scientist" may be needed. *Daubert* challenges, in brief, are challenges to the admissibility of expert testimony based on Fed. R. Evid. 702, which caused the court to subject proposed expert testimony to a factors analysis: (1) Was it subjected to peer-reviewed publication? (2) Does it have a known or knowable error rate? (3) Is it generally accepted in the relevant scientific field? (4) Has it been tested or is it testable? (*Daubert v. Merrill Dow Pharmaceuticals, Inc.*, 509 U.S. 579 (1993).) The fact that *Daubert* applies to "technical or other specialized knowledge" under Fed. R. Evid. 702, as well as to "scientific" knowledge, is the question answered in *Kumho Tire Co., Ltd. v. Carmichael, 526 U.S. 137 (1999). For a state supreme court opinion that foreshadows the Kumho Tire* decision, see *Gammill v. Jack Williams Chevrolet, Inc.*, 1998 Tex. Lexis, 22-23 (July 3, 1998). (See Section G.5., *infra*.)

A number of post-*Daubert* cases have suggested additional criteria to be evaluated in assessing reliability of expert testimony and methodology, and the decisions emanating from the district or circuit in which your case is filed should certainly be analyzed to determine the standards which may be applied. (See, generally, Section G, *infra.*) Considerations such as internal consistency, logical derivation from previously accepted methods, ability to account for all significant empirical data, and the credentials of the experts specially relating to utilization of this methodology have all been found to be pertinent. Courts have also looked to the quantitative and qualitative adequacy of the data utilized. (Good tests of only three bolts from a failed mechanism may be quantitatively inadequate although qualitatively adequate; hundreds of interviews which were all of young children, out-of-court and unsupervised, may be quantitatively adequate and qualitatively unacceptable.)

A.10. Emphasize differences between your case and your opponent's by highlighting the differences in credentials, approach, and style between your expert and your opponent's expert.

For example, if your expert has written in the area before having been hired, or considered a number of methodologies before selecting the best one for this case, while the other expert did not, then highlight these differences. Look for such differences regarding choice of methodology where a conclusion may have been reached prematurely, or thoroughness may have been lacking in considering all the important facts. Differences in style between experts can be used to emphasize differences in opinions. In other words, if their expert speaks only from the witness chair, does not use visual aids, and flaunts his specialized vocabulary, make certain that your expert is out of the chair often, uses interesting charts and pictures, and speaks in language that is understandable to the judge and jury.

B. Feeding an Expert

B.1. The expert must be the one who decides what information to consider and what to ignore.

Fed. R. Evid. 703 makes it clear that the bases for expert testimony must be information which is considered reliable by persons working in that field. The attorneys cannot select the information to funnel to the expert, because they are not competent to determine whether particular material should be relied upon or rejected. If the material for potential consideration is voluminous, then prepare an index or catalog for the expert to use as a menu from which to select, or request that the expert come to the location where the material is stored and conduct whatever review or examination is sufficient to allow him to make a selection. In response to the question at deposition or cross-examination, "Who selected the information that you considered?," you want the expert to be able to say, "I did."

B.2. Keep your written communications with the expert to a minimum.

Fed. R. Civ. P. 26 requires the disclosure of the information which the expert "considered" as she came to her conclusions and opinions. You do not want the disclosure of your thoughts and suggestions to the expert during trial preparation to hinge upon the semantic argument about the meaning of "considered." Some courts protect work product even when an expert "considers" it, but others do not protect even "core" work product. (See Section B.4.) (It should be noted that the change to "considered" was made, at least in part, to broaden expert discovery from the scope it had when courts required the disclosure only of materials which the experts had "relied upon.")

B.3. Keep the expert's written communications with you to a minimum.

Once the expert has committed something to writing (paper or electronic), that writing may qualify as potential evidence, and it should not be destroyed without consideration of the principles regarding spoliation and obstruction of justice. On the other hand, there is no obligation that the expert send you writings about her progress, or musings, or devil's advocate thoughts. (Indeed, there is no requirement that the expert write anything other than the expert report, if that is required by your forum court.) Therefore, do not create the potential evidence to begin with, and it will not have to be explained two years later, when both you and the expert have forgotten why it made sense and did not diminish your case. (In this context, remember that deleted e-mail messages apparently live forever and can be retrieved by experts specializing in such things.)

B.4. Assume that whatever you tell the expert about the case is discoverable.

There is some dispute among courts about whether all communications with the expert on the case are discoverable, even if they reveal the attorney's mental processes and tactical or strategic thinking. Courts that provide protection for such information when it is disclosed to the expert, argue that it constitutes "core work product" and is therefore immune from disclosure absent some showing of good cause and need, under the work product doctrine. Other courts have said that protection for work product can be waived, just like other privileges, and disclosure to a testifying expert constitutes just such a waiver. In other words, according to those courts, if you want your work product protected, do not reveal it — to anyone. Since it is impossible with complete accuracy to predict how a particular judge will rule when faced with such a question, the best strategy is to disclose your work product only to your client and to your trial team — co-counsel, paralegals, non-testifying experts — and provide the testifying expert with information which he can consider and disclose in giving his opinions, without revealing your confidences.

B.5. Do not hide facts from the expert.

Experts operate in fear that attorneys will try to influence their opinions by failing to reveal facts which the attorneys consider to be adverse. The experts (and intelligent attorneys) would much rather know the bad facts, so that they can analyze them and perhaps find ways to explain how they are consistent with the opinions being given. Consider, for example, a construction delay case in which the expert testified on direct examination that the delay was caused by the failure of the sand-and-gravel company to have enough sand available to supply the concrete contractor's needs; unknown to the expert (until cross-examination) was a fact, supported by photographic evidence, that there was a pile of surplus sand on the site of the sand-and-gravel company's operations, throughout the construction period. The court struck the expert witness's direct testimony from the record.)

B.6. Handle the expert's bills promptly.

Do not collect several months of the expert's bills without paying them, in order to make your monthly bills to the client look smaller or more reasonable. The client will not be any happier when she receives three months of expert bills all at once. More importantly, the expert will not be happy to be funding the client's cash flow and will not be as willing to put in the necessary hours and to incur the expenses for travel and preparation if reimbursement is a long time coming.

B.7. Allow the expert to use her own support staff.

When experts need to conduct research on some point in their analysis for your case, it is much more convenient for them to use their graduate students or laboratory assistants, rather than ask your paralegals or technical assistants to do the work. Using her own staff allows the expert to keep track of them, and it also makes it easier for her to testify that this underlying data or research by her assistants is reliable and of a type that is routinely relied upon in the particular field. She cannot say the same about work done by your paralegals, even if it seems rudimentary to you (like searching for relevant data compilations from the Bureau of the Census). On the other hand, there is nothing wrong with having your team respond to particular requests from an expert for identifiable data that can be collected without having to make judgments about relevance or utility.

B.8. Experts may have to reveal similar engagements, absent protective order.

There is no privilege automatically attached to other work being done by an expert, especially if that work relates in some way to the tasks in your case. Thus, an economist could be asked about analyses of competitive conditions in this or other markets, for other clients, to determine whether his notions of competition are consistent from case to case and market to market. Problems can arise if the expert has signed a confidentiality agreement, or is subject to a confidentiality order, in another case or engagement, and therefore declines to answer questions about that work. If you have anticipated this problem and asked the expert about the possibility, then you can ask the court for a protective order, arguing that the confidential information of that other client should not be disclosed in your case, and that the expert should not be precluded from earning a living by being foreclosed from maintaining confidences. You may need to notify the other client of the expert so that she can decide whether to send her own lawyers to argue for protection of her confidential information. After all, she is not your client, and as a technical matter you have no actual standing to assert her privileges or confidences.

B.9. Keep the non-testifying expert separated from the testifying expert.

The non-testifying expert may have very good ideas about ways to present and win the case. However, if he communicates those ideas directly to the testifying expert, then the non-testifying expert may become part of the basis for the testifying expert's opinions. As such, the non-testifying expert might be subject to deposition and other discovery. The primary purpose in hiring a non-testifying expert is to assist, inform, and educate you. Let the non-testifying expert share his ideas with you, and you can then present those ideas in an appropriate form to the testifying expert. Suppose, for example, that the non-testifying expert has identified a reason for using a different interest rate in discounting future income to its present value. If he communicates that directly to the testifying expert, she can fairly be asked where she obtained the information, or why she considered it, and the non-testifying expert winds up in the thick of discovery. If instead the non-testifying expert tells you of the different approach, you could discuss it with the testifying expert and allow the testifying expert to decide whether that information should be obtained (by a graduate student assistant) and considered. This is slightly more cumbersome, but it does reduce the possibility that the opinions of the testifying expert will be influenced by the non-testifying expert, who will therefore have to reveal that non-testifying expert's participation. (Yes, the graduate student who provides the data may be deposed, if an opposing party believes that the possibility of data error or manipulation, for example, justifies the expense.)

B.10. Confidentiality does not depend upon whether the expert contracts with the client or with the attorney.

Some lawyers have the expert enter a service contract directly with the lawyer or law firm, instead of with the client, on the belief that this provides an additional basis for claiming that communications with the expert are privileged or within the protection of the work product doctrine. Case law does not support this distinction. Legally and logically, the application of some privilege or protection for portions of the expert's work should depend upon what work is being done at whose direction; the source of information being considered; and the need of the opposing party for access to that information in order to have a fair opportunity to meet the expert's testimony. The completely formal fact of whether the contract is with the attorney or the client relates to none of these controlling considerations.

B.11. Insist that the expert visit the "evidence war room" and handle the documentary and real evidence.

After the expert has worked with materials that she has selected through your indices or otherwise and therefore has some familiarity with the kinds of documents and real evidence available, invite her to come to town to spend some time in the war room with the remainder of the material. One of your team members, or you, can give the expert a tour, and orient her while she goes through sample boxes (selected by her, of course). Dual purposes are served here: the expert increases her comfort level in saying that she has looked at all materials relevant to her analysis; and you are creating a scene that you will eventually want the jury to hear about ("Yes, well, then I spent three days with my sleeves rolled up, going through the boxes of material, to make certain for myself that there was nothing that we had overlooked, nothing that could make a difference, nothing that would point in another direction.") This is such a nice picture that you should actually take a photograph of your expert, sleeves rolled up, as she lifts documents out of an open box among several dozen. Indeed, why not put together a PowerPoint® storyboard showing the physical steps in the expert's analysis, so that the jury can appreciate that this was a hard job, well done?

C. Expert Reports

C.1. Most district courts are applying the provisions of Fed. R. Civ. P. 26(a)(2)(B) to govern expert disclosure; in some that are not, the individual judge has discretion to impose those provisions.

The December 2000 rule amendments should result in greater uniformity across the districts and circuits regarding the scope and manner of expert disclosures, through reports and depositions. ("Opting-out" is no longer so available for the courts.) Even if the various districts adopted identical, written pretrial orders, there would remain differences in each court because of different attitudes toward enforcement. Nevertheless, the intolerable situation where courts opted in or out of different discovery provisions should be eliminated, and we may be one step closer to a time when all lawyers can learn one set of rules for practicing in federal courts throughout the system.

C.2. Where an expert report is required, the report must be the work of the expert.

It is proper to inquire at deposition about the process leading to the production of the expert report. If the attorneys have participated too actively, not just by reviewing and correcting drafts, but by suggesting additional paragraphs or sections or by controlling or creating portions of the substantive contents of the report, a court may strike portions of the report, strike all of the report and require the preparation of a new report, or strike the report and preclude the expert from testifying. The attorneys should remember that while they may help the expert decide *how* to express an opinion, it is the expert's responsibility to decide *what* that opinion is. This is the same distinction as that between *preparing* a lay witness and *suborning perjury from* a lay witness. A lawyer may suggest answers and testimony, but only to the extent that the lawyer reasonably believes that the witness is not lying. (See, e.g., D.C. Bar Opinion 79.)

Note also that this may soon become a matter of professional ethics, at least for damages experts. A committee of damages experts is now at work with the ABA to draft a set of guidelines for damages experts in order that they preserve their professional objectivity and thereby their usefulness to the court. One of the main issues is to define the extent that a lawyer can assist an expert in preparing her report. While the expert must be the principal author and sign the report, Fed. R. Civ. P. 26 allows counsel to assist in its preparation by going over drafts and suggesting changes.

While the Advisory Committee to the Rules recognizes that there are times that the expert may legitimately need the lawyer's assistance in drafting her report, these are clearly limited to situations where the expert's stock in trade is brake repairs, stairway carpentry, or sewage management, presuming that these are professions requiring less facility with the written word. Where instead the expert is an econometrician who has written seven texts, forty-three articles, and three romance novels, her need for the lawyer's help in writing her report is less apparent. To be more blunt, such assistance was not intended to be permitted.

C.3. The parties can stipulate that expert reports are not required.

Fed. R. Civ. P. 26(a)(2)(B) specifically states, "[e]xcept as otherwise stipulated ... this disclosure shall ... be accompanied by a written report. ..." Fed. R. Civ. P. 29 grants the parties the power to stipulate to virtually all of the conditions governing discovery in their case, so long as the stipulated changes do not interfere with certain court-imposed deadlines and schedules. If the parties agree that they do not want to exchange expert reports, then there is a legitimate subject for stipulation. If you believe that your expert will make a superior presentation on direct examination, or that your expert will be more effective than the opposing expert at deposition, then the requirement to supply the other side with a report works against you, and avoiding expert reports may act in your favor.

C.4. Expert reports under Fed. R. Civ. P. 26(a)(2)(B) are hearsay for which there is no recognized exception.

Expert reports are statements which are prepared out of court and which, if offered, would be offered for the truth of the contents. They therefore come within the classic definition of hearsay. Nevertheless, some courts seem to accept these reports in evidence routinely, as though the requirement under Fed. R. Civ. P. 26 that reports be prepared were equivalent to an exception to the rule excluding hearsay. As a practical matter, if the opponent is willing to submit the expert's direct examination as a written report, the expert may have less impact, and the cross-examination may be easier, because the target is not moving. However, the physical report, if received in evidence, would normally go to the jury room, and that might give it more substance than the jury's recollected testimony of the other expert. Clearly, then, if one report is in, both should be in. If your opponent offers the report and it is admitted, and then she attempts to cover the same ground with live testimony, then you might consider an objection to cumulative evidence. "Once is enough," should be the rule, and the court may well be receptive. Remember, however, that your expert will be subject to the same rules that you succeed in imposing on the other expert.

C.5. Absent stipulation or court order, the primary expert reports are due not later than 90 days before trial, and rebuttal expert reports are due 30 days after the report which they rebut.

Fed. R. Civ. P. 26(a)(2)(C).

C.6. Expert reports must be supplemented to correct errors or omissions no later than 30 days before trial.

Fed. R. Civ. P. 26(a)(2)(C), 26(e)(1), and 26(3)(C). This is the same process which applies to expert depositions. (Parties have no duty to supplement their deposition responses, although they may of course make corrections to them, "in form or substance." Fed. R. Civ. P. 30(e). Parties do have a duty to supplement responses to interrogatories, requests for admission, and requests for production of documents.)

Counsel who tries to use a computer-generated model at trial which was produced by an expert to "supplement" or better explain his testimony, without first disclosing it as part of the expert's report, will logically be barred from using it by rules requiring that experts supplement their reports.

C.7. If a "rebuttal" expert report substantially or unfairly changes the substance of the expert's testimony as disclosed in the principal expert report, then the rebuttal expert report or testimony relating to the opinions disclosed in it could be excluded by the court.

There have been instances where counsel attempted to sandbag the opposition by reserving disclosure of the significant expert opinions until the filing of a "rebuttal" report, so that the opposition would not have the time or opportunity to conduct discovery on those opinions. The courts have a number of tools to deal with such conduct, including striking the report and precluding rebuttal by the expert or by the party.

In the face of a substantially revised "rebuttal" report, a party is certainly justified in asking for additional deposition time (even if it has to be at night during final trial preparations). If, during the deposition, you can extract information that shows that the expert has changed her opinions, or added to them, or altered her bases in a serious way, you could present that information to the court in a motion *in limine*, asking that the expert be precluded from voicing any opinions or relying on any bases that were not described in the original report and deposition.

C.8. The inclusion of material in an expert report does not preclude questioning on that and related material at deposition.

It was the hope of the drafters that sufficiently detailed expert reports would reduce the length of time spent in expert depositions. No figures are available to demonstrate whether this hope has been realized, although it seems unlikely, because of the trial lawyer's love of a good deposition. In any event, it was hoped that such a reduction would occur because the discovering party found that it needed less time at a deposition, not because areas revealed in the expert reports would therefore be off limits to further discovery. By the same token, the exclusion of information in an expert report — for example, failing to identify cases in which the expert has given testimony beyond the past four years — the period of disclosure required by the rule — does not create a "privilege from discovery" for that earlier testimony.

C.9. A party's regular employee who is presented as an expert is nevertheless "retained or specially employed" to provide expert testimony and must therefore author an expert report under the rules.

While the language of Fed. R. Civ. P. 26(a)(2)(B) is less than clear on this point, the concept is simple enough: a party cannot evade the obligation to make expert disclosures, including an expert report, by designating a regular employee as its expert and then claiming that he was not "retained or specially employed" for that purpose. While courts have differed, the better ruling is that if the employee does not regularly provide expert testimony for the party, he is retained or specially employed for the purpose; and if he does regularly provide expert testimony, he is covered by the later language of the rule, referring to employees "whose duties . . . regularly involve giving expert testimony. . . ."

C.10. The expert report shall contain a complete statement of opinions, bases, information considered, exhibits to be used as summaries or support, qualifications, publications within the past ten years, compensation, and trial or deposition testimony within the past four years.

Fed. R. Civ. P. 26(a). The "completeness" of this statement can be tested at the deposition of the expert. If there are serious deficiencies in the voluntary disclosures relating to expert information, orders to compel disclosures and to impose sanctions are available under Fed. R. Civ. P. 37, just as though there had been a failure to make discovery through interrogatories, requests for admission or production, or depositions.

C.11. The rule requires that the expert report contain information on testimony during the past four years and publications within the past ten years; nevertheless, interrogatories and depositions can request information about testimony and publications beyond those periods.

As mentioned in C.8, above, and D.2, below, other discovery devices may be used to obtain more information about the expert than is required in voluntary disclosures or expert reports. Especially with complex expert topics, like economics or psychology, where schools of thought may shift more often than in the fields of engineering or statistics, a more complete history of the expert's activities may be useful. For example, an antitrust economist may not have worked on anything similar to the instant case within the past four years, largely because the cases are so complex that they take five years to develop. But, she may have worked on two other very similar cases ten and fifteen years ago, and that knowledge may aid the cross-examiner. Remember that this rule, requiring disclosure in the expert's report, does not create a privilege protecting other matters from disclosure.

D. Non-Deposition Discovery About an Expert

D.1. Use graduate students in the field to investigate the opposing expert's credentials, publications, and prior testimony.

Your expert can help you identify graduate students who will identify, retrieve, and review the opposing expert's writings and prior testimony and check his claimed credentials. Graduate students understand the issues in the field and are available to work for less pay per hour than the least expensive law firm paralegal.

D.2. Use computerized legal research tools to check on prior testimony.

Once the expert has been identified, there is no need to accept the ten-year limit on the voluntary disclosure of publications or the four-year limit on testimony. Check the legal and scientific research databases to determine whether there are additional publications or testimony farther back. That earlier testimony might reveal changes in the expert's approach or opinions, or help you determine whether changes in client association result in changes in philosophy, e.g., did the antitrust economist develop more faith in free market forces after he left the government enforcement agency and began testifying for private industry?

D.3. Check to see whether the expert advertises that she is available to provide expert testimony.

Check local yellow pages, bar journals, legal newspapers and periodicals, and law school magazines and alumni publications to determine whether the expert is aggressively selling her expert testimonial services to attorneys. Are the advertisements blatantly skewed toward one side ("Challenging a drug screening? Need your own independent expert? Call Dr. Wilma Flintstone for reliable support.")?

Of course, you can also ask about the possibility of such advertising at deposition, and you can ask for copies of that advertising in your requests for production. Don't forget that "professional notices" inserted by engineers or handwriting analysts or disability specialists in the programs for annual meetings of bar association groups are possible sources of statements about the way that the expert may handle new matters. As discussed in D.9, below, the Internet is another source of potentially useful self-promotion by an expert.

D.4. Ask your non-testifying expert what he knows about the opposing expert and, if it is appropriate, ask him to make inquiries in the expert community.

Your non-testifying expert may very well know the opposing expert. You should obtain that knowledge in an organized way by taking the time to ask your expert how the opposing expert would approach this assignment, what biases and prejudices would be active, what sources would be preferred, and so forth, always looking for differences between your testifying expert's approach and that of the opposing expert. Unless the relevant field is so small that your expert would be uncomfortable, have him (or his graduate student assistants) telephone or e-mail others in the field for their information about the opposing expert. The testifying expert can participate in this investigation also, but be certain that you do not encourage her to become so much of an advocate that her objectivity is compromised.

D.5. Get a head start on identifying Fed. R. Evid. 803(18) "reliable authorities" by searching for publications which refer to the opposing expert or which are authored by colleagues at his company or school.

You can lay the foundation for the substantive admission of authoritative treatises through judicial notice that they are recognized as authorities, through the testimony of your own expert, or through the recognition of treatises as authoritative by the opposing expert. Because this last means of laying foundation is especially effective, it is worth the time to plan ahead. If asked at deposition whether a particular publication is a reliable authority or accepted as authoritative, the well-prepared expert may say, "Portions of it are certainly authoritative, but you would have to direct me to the specific sections you are interested in." However, if the expert is shown a publication which cites him by name, and then asked whether this is a respected or reliable publication, his ego may get the best of his judgment and he may agree that it is reliable without qualification. (Of course, you still need to find useful information in the publication that is relevant to the matter at hand, but at least you have a start on the foundation.)

D.6. In addition to reviewing testimony from prior cases, talk to the attorneys who opposed the expert in those cases.

Ask them general questions about the expert's demeanor and apparent work ethic, and ask them specific questions about whether they identified areas of weakness that were not presented on cross-examination (since you will be able to obtain the cross-examination to analyze for yourself).

D.7. Try to obtain the exhibits used during the expert's testimony in prior cases.

People have preferred ways of telling stories, and those preferences do not change completely when the story changes. Therefore, the type of exhibits the opposing expert used in past cases will give you some indication of the type of exhibits she will use in your case, especially if the issues in the cases are closely related (market entry conditions, strength of materials, adequate warning, DNA identification). No matter what market she is analyzing, the expert is likely to consider many of the same factors and to display them graphically in similar ways, from case to case.

D.8. Search for seminars, speeches, or panels at which the expert is appearing and send someone or obtain the published remarks.

Through your experts or by contacting the relevant professional societies, you may be able to identify meetings at which the opposing expert is going to speak about issues at least marginally related to those in your case. If you can have someone attend without subterfuge, there is nothing improper about listening to the expert's public remarks. Trying to obtain admissions about your case during the question-and-answer session seems to cross the line, however.

D.9. Search the Internet for hits on the expert's name.

Some experts themselves, or the schools or companies with which they are affiliated, have web sites which provide information about faculty or personnel. (This is different from the legal database searches recommended above.) The expert's professional biography may be available at such a site, and it would be interesting to compare that biography with the credentials provided under Fed. R. Civ. P. 26(a). Does the strength of materials expert list "plastics" as his area of specialization on the Internet when your case is about metals?

D.10. Identify the peer-reviewed publications in the field and have them searched for relevant articles.

One of the *Daubert* criteria for admissibility of expert testimony is whether the methodology has appeared in a publication requiring peer-review of articles. You will be asking about this at the deposition of the expert, and probably in interrogatories. You can forearm yourself to deal with evasive or incomplete answers by developing your own list of relevant peer-reviewed publications with which to examine.

Let's look at how this scene plays out. If you have no knowledge about "peer-reviewed" publications before you depose the opposing expert, you will not be prepared to conduct follow-up examination when that expert mentions her readings in certain periodicals or treatises. On the other hand, if your expert or your research has provided you with the prominent journals in the field, you might come to the deposition with copies of the last five years' issues; then, when the expert says that her methodology must have been discussed in that magazine within the past few years, you can put them all in front of her and ask her, "Where?" If she finds it, that's good for you, because now you have a guide to what she should have done; if she does not find it, that's good, too, since it seems to remove "peer-reviewed publication" from the bases for reliability of her methodology. Of course, with the limit of one day applied to all depositions now, absent court order or stipulation, you must spend your time carefully; two hours for the expert to peruse forty magazines may be too much (but twenty minutes to look at the tables of contents of ten magazines may be time well spent).

E. Preparing an Expert to Be Deposed

E.1. If an expert report is required, then the deposition of an expert may only be conducted after the report is provided.

Fed. R. Civ. P. 26(b)(4). This schedule is consistent with the drafters' desire to avoid unnecessarily lengthy expert depositions by postponing the depositions until the voluntary disclosures have been made, including the expert reports. As a result, expert depositions are likely to occur within the last 90 days before trial. Many courts had already required that expert depositions be conducted at or after the close of all other discovery. (Under this rule, expert depositions may be taken as a matter of right; court permission is no longer required. Expert depositions had become common practice, and now the rule comports with reality.)

E.2. The expert may use notes during the deposition.

Where the expert's work and testimony are especially detailed or complex, there is no rule that the expert cannot have an outline, or a summary, or some other form of notes (such as an annotated copy of her report) in front of her while giving her deposition testimony. However, you must assume that those materials will be requested by, and eventually disclosed to, the other side. In fact, because they are so clearly related to the deposition testimony, a court will order the deposition resumed for further questioning if the notes are not provided at the time. The best approach, then, is to make certain that the notes are no more extensive than needed to remind the expert of a point or to direct the expert to an exception, example, or limitation. The notes will have to be disclosed at some point to the other side because it is clear from the context that the expert is using them to refresh her memory. Of course, it is fair to remind the witness that the notes need be no more complete than is necessary for the witness's purposes. So, for example, if the expert marks the number "5" in the margin of a report, in order to remind himself that the fifth item in a list is worth special consideration, then disclosure of that number itself does not provide much advantage to the questioning party.

The expert (or a lay witness) need not disclose documents that were reviewed during her preparation for the deposition, unless the foundation is laid that those documents refreshed her memory. This procedure has developed from analogy to trial conduct, where the opposing party is entitled to see anything used to refresh a witness's recollection, but is not entitled to see the collection of documents selected by counsel for preparation purposes, since that selection process itself is protected by the work product doctrine.

While the expert is normally not required to state which documents her counsel selected for special review in preparation for the deposition, that does not confer any privilege on those documents. If they were considered by the expert, then they must be identified in the expert report, and they must be produced in response to a request calling for the documents that the expert considered. Here we are merely pointing out that the subset of documents selected by the attorney for review for the deposition is not separately identifiable unless the expert agrees that those documents refreshed her recollection.

E.3. Try to reduce the witness's anxieties during preparation.

Less experienced expert witnesses may have the same anxieties about deposition testimony as lay witnesses. Therefore, advice like, "Don't let them trick you," or "Watch out for hostile attacks," does nothing other than raise the witness's anxieties about the whole process and distract them from their principal responsibility of answering the questions directly, truthfully, and briefly. Remind the witness of this responsibility during preparation sessions, and assure the witness that if anything comes up which she wants to discuss or which she does not understand, you will be right there, precisely for that purpose.

E.4. The "seven answers to most deposition questions" work for expert witnesses as well as lay witnesses.

Those answers are yes, no, green, I don't know, I don't remember, I don't understand the question, and I need a break. The emphasis is on truth and brevity; if the questioning attorney wants more information, he can always ask for it, but it is not efficient for the witnesses to try to guess where the attorney is going or what he wants. The answer "green" is an example of the proper response to a "small" question, like, "What color is your car?" The answer is not, "I have a '93 green Buick station wagon that I bought used." The answer is, "Green." All additional information merely invites the attorney to conduct follow-up until he is certain that "station wagon, '93, Buick, and used" contain no relevant information.

"I don't know" is the very best answer for the expert or lay witness when she does not know. Otherwise, if she says, "Yes, I know," the next question will be, "How do you know that?" and she's stuck. Tell the expert that she is not required to know everything; some things (like next year's interest rates) are unknowable; some things need to be looked up (the population of Ecuador); and some things are not relevant to the matter at hand (at least from the expert's perspective) and therefore were not worth knowing (whether the driver was going to the grocery store or the school when the rack-and-pinion steering mechanism failed, from the point of view of the metallurgical engineer studying the stresses on the steering gear). Tell the expert that it is okay to say, "I don't know," when that is the correct answer.

"I don't remember" is a very good answer when the witness does not remember; the alternatives are to speculate (which, while allowed at deposition, introduces uncertainty and the serious possibility of error into the testimony) and to lie. Lying is not attractive.

The expert, like the lay witness, should be told that, "I don't understand the question" is a fair response, and the only appropriate response, when she in fact does not understand the question, either because it is defective in its form (compound, complex, ambiguous), because it is confusing in its context, antecedents or other predicates, or because the questioner has used words or phrases in a way that is not clear to the expert deponent. Often, when the words or phrases are familiar to the expert but their use in the particular context is confusing, the expert will be tempted to answer the question with her own question, like, "When you say 'force' in this question, do you really mean 'momentum,' since force is mass times acceleration and momentum is mass times velocity?" Such a response provides the questioner with additional choice points (Ask about momentum? Ask about the difference between velocity and acceleration? Ask whether that difference alters the expert's opinion?); and therefore extends the deposition. The expert's best response when she doesn't understand the question is to say, "I'm sorry; I don't understand your question," and then to let the questioner select another question. If the questioner asks, "What don't you understand?" the witness can say, "I don't understand what you mean by 'force' in your question." In preparation, the expert should be told that it is not sufficient that she understands the individual words that are used to ask the question; she should not answer unless she believes that she knows what the questioner means in asking the question.

There are times in every deposition when the witness is not certain what to do. There may be a question pending, or there may not. If the witness, for whatever reason, believes that she needs to take a break before going forward, then she should say, to you or to the questioner, "I would like to take a break now." And you should then take a break, no matter what protest the other side raises. You really have no choice, because you cannot go forward (that is, instruct the witness to continue with the deposition) until you find out what is on her mind. It may something trivial ("I didn't understand his use of the word "heteroskedasticity," but I didn't know how to point out my difficulty"), or it may be something more serious ("I am concerned that, if I answer this question about other engagements I currently have, I may be violating a confidentiality agreement I signed in another case"), but until you know about it you cannot provide competent counsel to the expert witness. These are clear examples of why the draconian rules in some districts restrict communication between counsel and witness during a deposition go too far, at least when one is dealing with attorneys who are also grown-ups. Take a break when the witness asks for one; find out the reason for the break; and deal with it ethically and honestly; if it is necessary to put something on the record about the break ("The witness recalled that she had a conference call scheduled for this next half hour, but we have called and moved it"), then do so and ask counsel to re-ask the question.

E.5. Before the expert's list of credentials is turned over under Fed. R. Civ. P. 26(a), review it in detail with the expert, asking for an explanation of each entry.

It is very likely that this review will be conducted by opposing counsel as part of the deposition, so you should be certain that the expert (and you) will not be embarrassed by the answers. Honorary degrees should be identified as such; co-authored works, or edited works, should identify co-authors or editorship; non-exclusive memberships should be omitted; professional and educational affiliations and background should be stated precisely and accurately.

E.6. Prepare the expert for attempts to lay foundation for "learned treatises."

Under Fed. R. Evid. 803(18), if a work is established as a reliable authority by the testimony of the opposing expert witness (or by judicial notice or testimony of one's own expert witness), then relevant portions may be read into the record as substantive evidence. The foundation is essentially two-pronged: the writing is shown to be a reliable authority, and the material to be read is relevant. During expert depositions, it is proper to ask the expert whether there are authorities in the field which he considers reliable, or which are considered reliable by others in the field. If he identifies some works as reliable authorities, then the opposing attorney may review them before trial and be prepared on cross-examination to introduce portions which either contradict some part of the expert's direct testimony or support some part of the opposing party's case (Fed. R. Evid. 106 allows opposing or clarifying portions to be included on motion request.). When confronted with a request at deposition to identify reliable authorities, the expert's best answer, if true, is, "There are several good works out there, but I would have to know what exact point you are interested in to tell you whether a particular book or article is reliable for that purpose." When one expert was asked whether he considered his own book reliable, he answered, "I believe that 50 percent of it is absolutely correct; I just can't decide which 50 percent." (See, also, Section D.5.)

E.7. Seek a protective order if you want to try to protect information about the expert's related engagements.

As discussed above in Section B.8., work that the expert is doing for other clients may be very useful to the opposing party in determining whether the expert's analysis in this case is consistent or is result-oriented. That other work normally comes within no recognized privilege (although there is the unusual situation where the expert is in a privileged relationship with another client, as might happen with a medical or legal expert). Nevertheless, the expert may want to keep the details of that work, and perhaps the relationship itself, confidential. The burden is on the party seeking to prevent disclosure to seek a protective order, and that order should be obtained before the deposition, so that the deposition is not interrupted and the deposing party put to wasted time and expense.

E.8. Explain the relevant law, including *Daubert*, to the expert.

Experts need to know whether their opinions are going to judged by particular legal standards that they might not be accustomed to dealing with. For example, if a medical expert will be required to testify "to a reasonable degree of medical certainty," she needs to know whether this means that her opinion has to be based on a scientific standard in medical research, or whether it means only that, in her professional judgment, she holds her opinion as being "more likely true than not." This detail may require some preparation time to make sure the witness understands the standard and is comfortable with testifying under the required standard.

Of course *Daubert* ought to be raised sooner rather than later with your expert. Knowing that a *Daubert* challenge is possible, it should be an easy matter for the expert to document the analysis along the way with authoritative texts and detailed working papers.

E.9. Review the most helpful and the most harmful documents with the expert witness.

The witness may have concerned herself primarily with statistical data, government reports, or other "objective" data. At deposition, however, she will be asked about memoranda from the client which are claimed as support for the client's position, or which are seen by the opposing party as contradicting that position. The expert should be familiar with the most important of these documents, and with the responsibilities of the people involved in creating or receiving the documents. While the expert may have to consider hundreds or thousands of pages of data, it is unlikely that more than a few dozen text documents will be significant. (This, for the same reasons, underlies our rule of thumb that there are no more than fourteen documents on which a jury or judge makes a decision: Faced with complex questions and problems, human beings try to simplify, categorize, and summarize; a clear document is allowed to stand for all similar but less clear documents; peripheral issues and disputes are resolved after, and consistently with, the decision in the main dispute; global documents and summaries are utilized in place of individual records. We cannot comprehend or manipulate all of the information presented by hundreds or thousands of documents, so, we select a few to stand for the many.)

E.10. Remind the expert not to be an overt advocate.

You want the jury to believe that your expert has been objective and relatively independent. If, during deposition or trial testimony, the expert refuses to concede reasonable points or to recognize limitations or exceptions to her conclusions, then her credibility will be diminished. It is *not* necessary that the expert volunteer exceptions to her opinions at deposition; it *is* necessary that she identify, for herself and you, the core elements of her analysis, and save her "to the death" defense for those elements, being reasonably flexible in her discussions of other aspects of the analysis. Where the expert's deposition is being videotaped for possible use at trial, the appearance of objectivity is even more important. Again, while it is better to have this discussion earlier rather than just before the deposition, if the expert is uncomfortable giving an opinion on a matter because it is out of his area of expertise, it is better for the expert to admit that fact (and get a second, supplementary expert) than to make your single expert lose credibility by trying to do too much.

A second reason to present an "objective" approach is that your expert might need to persuade the opposing lawyer (and client) that you have good case. In a day when most cases settle, you should recognize that your expert can be a positive force toward fair settlement of the case. To the extent that you persuade the other lawyer and opponent that your expert has looked carefully and fairly at the facts, you advance a good settlement outcome for your client.

In this regard, you should help the expert to articulate his main opinions in brief and clear language, thinking all of the time about how those statements will sound if read in front of the jury. "The defendants engaged in price-fixing," is a better statement than, "Based upon what I have seen, I have come to the conclusion, with which I am reasonably comfortable, that the defendants, at least for the period of a few years, coordinated their pricing behavior, both through overt agreements and implicit interdependent decisions, so as to avoid the effects of direct competition along that dimension." The first statement of opinion also comports with the general rule for deposition answers, discussed above, that they should be brief and truthful. Although it may seem that it is tactically better to require the opposing party to dig and dig to obtain all of the expert's opinions, there is a risk that the expert will forget some portion of his analysis or state subsidiary opinions in a way which conflicts with other opinions.

E.11. Prepare the expert to make an affirmative statement of her opinion in response to your follow-on questioning, so that you have that testimony available for motions practice.

Since so many cases today are resolved through motions or settlement before trial, we must recognize that an important goal in taking and defending depositions is to obtain material that can be used to support motions for summary judgment or other motions to limit the case. It is fair that witnesses are not allowed to create declarations which vary their deposition testimony substantially, in order to avoid the effect of admissions they may have made at deposition; it makes much more sense for the expert to speak out, at the deposition, if her opinions have not been fairly portrayed or if they are being excluded from the record by procedural ploys ("Dr. Smith, I understand that you might want to explain your methods, but I am really not interested in that explanation now; just answer, yes or no, whether you looked at 1990 Census data").

E.12. Remember that the burden of showing "reliability" in a *Daubert* context is on the proponent; therefore, a trial or preservation deposition of an expert should contain at least a *prima facie* show-

ing of reliability, using several of the four *Daubert* criteria or other indicia of reliability.

In the infrequent case that your expert cannot be available for trial, and you therefore conduct a *de bene esse* deposition to preserve that testimony for later use, or where your expert travels extensively, is of advanced age or poor health, or for some other reason may become unavailable for trial, remember that the burden is on you, the proponent of the expert's testimony, to demonstrate at trial that the deposition testimony presents opinions achieved through the application of reliable methodologies; that is foundational, just as it would be foundational to show (from the deposition itself, or from the testimony of another witness) that the deposition testimony of a witness to a car accident came from someone with firsthand, or percipient, knowledge (that is, that the absent witness was in a position to see, was capable of seeing, and was testifying about what he saw). The absence of such information about the reliability of the expert's methodologies, from the deposition or other source, would be fatal to the offer of the expert's testimony, because the proponent has the burden of persuading the judge (not the jury at this stage, because this is a question of admissibility) that the opinions in the deposition testimony are the product of reliable methodologies capably employed. (See Rule F.1, below.)

F. Deposing Expert Witnesses

F.1. Ask an expert witness these ten questions at deposition, even if you don't have time to ask anything else:

(a) What opinions have you formed in this matter?

(b) What did you do to reach those opinions?

(c) How did you do that?

(d) Why did you do that?

(e) What result did you get?

(f) How did that result affect your opinion?

(g) Are there reliable authorities in this field?

(h) What assumptions did you make in your work?

(i) What tasks didn't you do?

(j) Is this your current and accurate resume?

One caveat: You may be tempted by an ambush strategy to look at an expert's report for things that they have left out — a key area of necessary qualifications, the absence of evidence that they can meet the *Daubert* standard, or no mention of the requisite legal standard. You may think it better to choose not to depose on these areas at the deposition and bring these omissions up at a pretrial hearing. (Some courts, like Texas, will require you bring up *Daubert* objections pretrial, in order to preserve them for appeal.) You may decide to surprise your opponent at pretrial with your *Daubert* challenge, rather than put him on notice of the witness's failings in time for the expert to supplement his report for trial. You may think that at the pretrial it may be too late for the plaintiff to rebut the challenge and the witness may be barred from testifying, which may allow you to succeed on a motion to dismiss. Note, however, that the parties are allowed to supplement testimony at Fed. R. Civ. P. 104 conferences with affidavit testimony, just as one can in a summary judgment motion. If the witness will be allowed to supplement his testimony with an affidavit, then it is probably a better strategy to ask the witness about gaps in his opinion before he will have a chance to talk with opposing counsel. In other words, trial by ambush often does not work. It is better to test your theories in the deposition, so that you are not surprised by the response when it is too late to rebut. If, however, no such supplementation will be allowed, then your silence on such *Daubert* points at the deposition may be appropriate.

However, where the parties have agreed to videotape the expert's deposition for purposes of trial, the decision is much different. Where the deposition is conducted to preserve the expert's testimony for trial, the proponent of the expert has an affirmative burden to put on sufficient evidence that establishes their expert case. If they do not do so, then you might chose not to ask questions and then move for dismissal or for summary judgment. (See *Celotex v. Catrett*, 477 U.S. 317 (1986) and F.5. below.)

F.2. Ask, "What did you review or consider and decide not to rely on?"

There was a time when courts would not allow discovery of materials which the experts had reviewed but had not used as a basis for their opinions. The rationale was probably twofold: if the expert did not use the material in coming to his opinion, then it was believed to be of limited relevance; and there was probably enough material that the expert did use so that not much was being lost by this restriction. Nowadays, the courts are much more reasonable in allowing inquiry on deposition and cross-examination into the expert's decision not to use, consider, or rely upon certain materials. After all, if the expert has created two piles of documents labeled "Stuff that I like " and "Stuff that I don't like," then the cross-examiner may be much more interested in the stuff which the expert did not like.

F.3. Ask "Who in this field agrees with your methodology? Who disagrees?"

The expert may be an outlier in this particular area of dispute, so that other experts are arrayed against her. If the expert identifies some others who disagree with her methodology, then ask for their names and whatever details she can provide about the basis for their disagreements. If the expert identifies other experts who agree with her, then pursue that information to set up examination under Fed. R. Evid. 803(18): there may be materials that they have written which disagree with or at least limit the approach that she has taken. Therefore, ask whether any of these other experts are considered to be reliable authorities (or, more correctly, whether their work is considered to be reliable, although the courts do not always make this rather fine distinction). Then, have your expert and the graduate student assistants review the works of these experts in relevant areas to see if they can find something to be used on cross-examination as impeachment or as substantive evidence.

F.4. Ask, "Who selected the materials which you reviewed? Did you ask for anything that you did not receive?"

Occasionally, you will find that an attorney will pack up a bundle of apparently relevant materials and send them off to the expert without telling the expert that there is more or that the expert is free to request additional information. This is a very bad position to put the expert in, because it leaves him open to cross-examination which asks, "Who sent you those materials? Did you tell them what you wanted? Were you aware that there were additional materials on this subject which were not shown to you? Had you been aware of those additional materials, would you have liked the opportunity to see them before you formed your opinion and gave testimony under oath?" If you are lucky enough, you may one day depose an expert who admits that he asked for some materials that he did not receive. Then you can ask on cross-examination, "Who decided that you wouldn't receive those materials? Was that your decision, as the expert in this case, or was that the lawyer's decision?"

F.5. Ask the *Daubert* questions of the opposing expert at deposition.

There is no specific formulation of these questions, but the following examples provide guidance:

(a) Has this methodology appeared in a peer-reviewed publication?

(b) What is the error rate attributable to this methodology? (Is it known or knowable?)

(c) Has this methodology achieved general acceptance in the relevant scientific field?

(d) Is this methodology testable when used for these purposes — that is, are the results replicable?

(e) Was this methodology created for the purposes of this litigation?

This last question was actually added by the Ninth Circuit after the Supreme Court remanded the original *Daubert* case for further proceedings. The first four, which can be remembered by use of the acronym "PEAT," for peer, error, acceptance, and testability, are directly from the Supreme Court's opinion. The courts and commentators have also analyzed this decision as establishing two criteria, rather than four, for the admissibility of expert testimony: relevance (or fit) and reliability. Of course, all testimony must be relevant to be admissible, but with experts this "fit" concept asks specifically whether the expert's opinion testimony will be helpful to the judge or jury. Reliability is another way of referring to the four criteria mentioned above. ("Relevance and reliability" are one way to summarize the foundation needed for the admission of any evidence, so there is nothing strikingly new here.) Other courts have added additional criteria to this list, as they were encouraged to do by the Supreme Court. The four (or five or more) conditions are neither necessary nor sufficient; that is, their presence does not guarantee admissibility nor their absence foreclose it — other criteria may preclude or support it.

There are other criteria which assist in determining whether the expert's methodologies are reliable, such as those discussed in "The *Daubert* Deposition Dance: Retracing the Intricacies of the Expert's Steps."[2] These include the quantitative and qualitative sufficiency of the data employed, the consistency of the specific approach with the general methodology, the logical derivation of the methodology, and the ability of the proponent expert to articulate a clear and logical relationship between the methodology and the resulting opinion.

F.6. Identify the assistants who collected, calculated, or considered information.

Busy experts use lab or office assistants and graduate students to do much of the legwork for their engagements. Depending upon the complexity of the assignment, that work may involve important decisions and choices which influence the ultimate outcome, calculation, or opinion. If you find that

---

2. Malone, David M. and Ryan M. Malone, *Journal of the North Carolina Trial Lawyers' Association* (September, 2000), reprinted herein at page 101 with permission of the copyright holders.

the work of the assistants possibly had an influence on the opinion, depending upon its accuracy or the selections of data, then you may be able to justify depositions of those assistants. It is common, for example, for the primary expert to have very little competence or information regarding the computer program used to generate the results of regression analyses used in econometric, statistical, and epidemiological work. In such a case, the accuracy of that work can only be examined by questioning the junior expert who actually worked with the computer programs and data.

F.7. Identify all of the opinions and then go back and identify the bases for each opinion one at a time.

You ask the expert, "What opinions have you reached?" and he answers, "I have formed an opinion that the steering mechanism on the tanker truck was defectively designed and manufactured." You are greatly tempted at that point to ask what, why, how, when — all to identify the bases for that opinion. The problem with giving in to that temptation is that you may forget to come back and ask about any other opinions; and, if you do remember later on, there may not be enough time to treat those other, potentially more important, opinions and bases as fully as they ought to be treated. Instead, have the expert identify all of the opinions he has formed in this matter: "Have you reached any other opinions? Are there more opinions that you hold in this case? Are those three opinions all of the opinions you have on the causes of the accident? Are there any materials which might remind you of other opinions?" Once you have a complete list of his opinions, go back to the first (or whichever you consider the most important, having heard them all), and explore the bases for that opinion.

F.8. Do not assume that you know the answer to any question.

Experts are ordinarily the most educated, most intelligent witnesses we confront. If we assume, at a deposition, that we already know what they are going to answer in particular areas, we may be surprised and embarrassed at trial. At the expert deposition, start broadly and narrow the areas covered only as you gather evidence that the excluded areas are not relevant. You can gain the expert's help in this process by asking at the outset, "Tell us how you saw this assignment at the beginning of your engagement. What areas did you think about investigating? What aspects of engineering were involved, as you saw the project then? When did you begin to narrow your inquiry or analysis? How did you do that? Why did you do that?" By questions such as these, you are learning how the witness narrowed the field of inquiry, rather than assuming that you already know how and to what it was narrowed.

F.9. Be the expert's most interested, but ignorant, student.

Ordinarily, the goal of a deposition is not to display how much you know about the expert's field; it is to find out what he knows and what he did with respect to matters important to your case. If the expert and his counsel leave the deposition room believing that you are ignorant in the field of metallurgy or medical statistics, but you have learned everything about what the expert will say at trial, and why, you are better off than they. Therefore, do not worry about appearing ignorant at the deposition by asking basic questions, by asking for explanations, and by asking for the definitions of terms. If you ask such questions with animation, if you are leaning forward in your chair, if you have good eye contact with the expert, if you pick up on phrases he uses and incorporate them in your questioning — in other words, if you do all those things that we do when we are truly interested in a speaker's subject — then the expert may lower his defenses and try to educate you. You will have become his most interested, albeit ignorant, student. Your lack of genuine interest — for example, in the vagaries of real estate accounting — should be no bar. Remember what George Burns said when, in his youth at age eighty-seven or so, he was asked, "Mr. Burns, you have spent eighty years on the stage. To what do you attribute your remarkable theatrical success?" "Sincerity," said Burns. "Once you learn to fake that, all the rest is easy."

F.10. Ask the expert to get up and use the black-board or whiteboard to explain her testimony.

Many experts who appear in court are also teachers; they enjoy the audience and the power — the spotlight. At deposition, take advantage of this inclination to teach by putting them in the teaching mode. You, after all, will be the one learning. Invite them to leave their chairs at the deposition table and to use whatever materials they need to explain their work and opinions. In all likelihood, you will be seeing a dress rehearsal of their trial testimony. Of course, during cross-examination at trial, you will not invite them to leave the witness chair to teach; they will have to stay in the chair and allow you to teach through your leading questions. That change in conduct only may frustrate them at trial and make them less sure of themselves.

F.11. Establish the existence and identity of learned treatises so that you may examine them and perhaps use them during cross-examination of this or another expert witness.

As discussed in E.6, above, you have prepared your own expert to respond to questions on whether there are reliable authorities which could be accepted as exceptions to the rule excluding hearsay, under Fed. R. Evid. 803(18). At the deposition of the opposing expert, you should ask about books she recommends, books written by colleagues in the same college department, articles she has used in advancing her own knowledge, publications she has found particularly useful in analyzing the kind of factors she is facing in the instant case. You will not know, as you obtain this information from her, what will be useful and what will not; that determination must await evaluation of the identified learned treatises by you or, more likely, your graduate student team members. Try to question the expert on these materials as though you were skeptical of her ability to name any such authoritative sources ("You certainly don't have time to keep up with important research and writing in your field, do you, considering all the time you spend teaching and consulting?"), so that her inclination is to volunteer more reliable sources than she otherwise would.

G. Admissibility of Expert Testimony

G.1. The Court determines the admissibility of expert testimony under Fed. R. Evid. 401, 701, and 702.

Fed. R. Evid. 401 requires that expert testimony (and any other material offered in evidence at trial) be relevant to be admissible. It also must be reliable, a requirement implicit in Fed. R. Evid. 702 and 703. In *Daubert*, the Supreme Court "replaced" the widely used *Frye* test (which required the bases for expert testimony to be "generally accepted in the relevant field" in order to establish reliability) with a four-prong test of reliability: (1) Has the methodology been subjected to **peer-reviewed publication**? (2) Is there a known or knowable **error rate** for the methodology? (3) Is the methodology generally **accepted** in the relevant scientific field? and (4) Has the methodology been **tested** or is it testable? We offer the acronym PEAT as a mnemonic device to help in remembering the Supreme Court's criteria. The Supreme Court invited lower courts to consider additional factors indicating reliability (or lack thereof), as they exercised their role as gatekeeper for expert evidence. The Ninth Circuit, on remand of the *Daubert* case, added the additional consideration of whether the methodology was created for the purposes of litigation, as opposed to having been developed in non-litigation applications in the relevant field. Various districts and circuits have added other criteria to this reliability analysis.

G.2. Objections to expert testimony are made by motion *in limine* before trial, by objection (based on *voir dire*, if requested and granted by the court) after the tender or the completion of the presentation of qualifications at trial, or by objection when the particular opinion is called for during testimony.

The motion *in limine* is appropriate when an adequate deposition record or other evidence has been compiled which will allow the court to make a judgment about whether the expert testimony meets the criteria of reliability and relevance, and when the opponent believes that it is especially important to attempt to keep the jury from hearing from the expert at all. As a practical matter, the judge will be more receptive to evaluating a complex question of admissibility when he is not faced with the pressure of having a jury waiting. *Voir dire* and objection make sense if the opponent has to develop some additional facts in order to demonstrate to the judge that the testimony should not be admitted. Questioning on *voir dire* also allows the opponent of the testimony to suggest to the jury that there are reasons to be skeptical of the expert's testimony, even if the judge overrules the objection after the *voir dire*. The same questioning could be postponed to cross-examination, if the opponent thinks it is unlikely to result in exclusion or limitation of the testimony, but at that point the jury will have heard the expert and perhaps been persuaded despite the deficiencies.

G.3. The *Daubert* criteria are to be applied to the expert's methodology, not to the expert's conclusions or opinions.

Courts should not reject expert testimony because the results are unexpected, contrary to the court's beliefs, or a departure from prior opinions or conclusions in the field. However, it is clear even from the *Daubert* opinion itself that a court should reject expert testimony if the conclusion is not rationally connected to the "reliable" methodology. Thus, an expert may reliably utilize an accepted methodology for determining the fullness of the moon on a particular date, but that reliable methodology will not permit the admission of the conclusion that a full moon rendered the criminal defendant insane at the time of the murder.

G.4. The *Daubert* approach to evaluating the reliability of expert testimony through examining appropriate criteria applies to all expert knowledge, whether it is classified as scientific, technical, or specialized.

In *Kumho Tire Co., Ltd. v. Carmichael*, 526 U.S. 137 (1999), the Supreme Court eliminated the confusion which had arisen in the circuit courts about whether there was a distinction to be made in the analysis of scientific testimony on the one hand, and technical and specialized testimony, on the other. In *Kumho*, the circuit court had reversed the trial court's rejection of expert mechanical engineering testimony based on *Daubert*-type analysis, saying that *Daubert* principles did not apply to the technical testimony being offered. In a unanimous decision reversing the circuit court, the Supreme Court also emphasized that the trial court's decisions on admissibility of expert testimony are to be reviewed under the normal "clear abuse of discretion" standard regardless of the field of expertise involved. The Court restated the approach in *Daubert* to clarify the obligation of trial courts and counsel to identify appropriate criteria for this reliability test because those criteria will vary from case to case and field to field, and cannot be exhaustively listed. For examples of the existence and handling of this scientific versus non-scientific dichotomy prior to the clarification in *Daubert, see Watkins v. Telesmith Inc.*, 121 F.3d 484, 491 (5th Cir. 1997); *Southland Sod Farms v. Stover Seed Co.*, 108 F.3d 1134, 1143 n.8 (9th Cir. 1997); *Peitzmeier v. Hennessy Indus. Inc.*, 97 F.3d 293, 297 (8th Cir. 1996)(cert. den. 520 U.S. 1196 (1997)); *Tyus v. Urban Search Management*, 102 F.3d 256, 263 (7th Cir. 1996), *but cf. Compton v. Suburu of America, Inc.*, 82 F. 3d 1513, 1519 (10th Cir. 1996).

G.5. After *Kumho Tire*, there is no need for a rule defining the distinction between scientific testimony and technical or specialized testimony.

The trial court should use the same approach for all experts in determining whether their expert knowledge is sufficiently reliable to be admitted in court. The four reliability criteria of *Daubert* (publication in peer-reviewed journals, known or knowable error rate, acceptance in the relevant scientific community, and testability or replicability by other researchers in the field), or other criteria found to be equally or more appropriate to a particular field, are to be used in each instance that such an analysis of reliability is required. Examples of such additional criteria, from *Kumho* and elsewhere, are: the extent to which the methodology explains the significant data; internal consistency of the methodology; the relation of the methodology to other methods already accepted as reliable; the quantitative and qualitative adequacy of the data utilized; the logical relationship between the methodology offered and methodologies that preceded it; the credentials of the expert.

G.6. Where admissibility is not clear, the proponent of expert testimony should seek a pretrial ruling through a motion *in limine*.

If the party offering the expert's testimony is unclear of the standards to be applied in ruling on admissibility, then it is dangerous to wait for the trial to find out how the judge will analyze the question. At trial, when the court decides that *Daubert* applies, it may be too late to lay the appropriate foundation. An alternative approach is to assume that *Daubert* applies, and to lay the more extensive foundation which that case requires for scientific testimony. However, it is unclear how the four primary *Daubert* criteria, as an example — obviously created with "hard" sciences in mind — would be applied to the testimony of an expert in the field of spousal abuse syndrome, political science, or cabinetmaking. Indeed, any witness who has obtained his expertise through training and experience rather than education, will have trouble satisfying the primary *Daubert* criteria, as will many others. A court might well adopt different criteria for different "scientific" disciplines, but, if that determination is not made until trial, then uncertainty about the admissibility of the expert's testimony will make preparation for trial virtually impossible.

G.7. At the deposition of the expert, the criteria for admissibility should be explored after the opinions are known.

The expert's basis for claiming that the *Daubert* and other criteria have been met should be explored at the deposition. If the defendant's expert can be forced to admit that some or many criteria are not satisfied, then the court is more likely to exclude the testimony than if the same argument is based only on the testimony of the plaintiff's expert.

G.8. At the deposition, analyze the opposing expert's testimony in terms of what the expert brought to the case on the one hand, and what the case gave to the expert on the other.

This dichotomy corresponds to Professor Imwinkelreid's[3] major and minor premises, and they also approximate the relative scope of Fed. R. Evid. 702 and 703, respectively. In trying to determine whether to make a challenge by motion *in limine*, on *voir dire*, by objection, or through cross-examination, it is generally true that inadequacy of credentials, irrelevance of the particular scientific discipline, or general unreliability of the methodology employed (which are all examples of failings in what the expert brought to the case) provide some possibility of excluding the expert's testimony entirely, and should therefore be raised as early as possible before trial. Challenges based on the adequacy of the data employed, errors in the calculations, or alternative data not considered are less likely to lead to overall exclusion and may be most effective on cross-examination.

---

3. Imwinkelreid, *The "Bases" of Expert Testimony: The Syllogistic Structure of Scientific Testimony*, 67 N.C. Law Rev. 1 (1987).

G.9. If the expert's report under Fed. R. Civ. P. 26(a)(2) does not adequately disclose her opinions and bases, there is a risk that the expert's testimony will be limited or even excluded.

The admissibility of the expert's testimony obviously depends not only upon its evidentiary reliability and relevance, but also upon whether the proponent has adequately satisfied the procedural obligations imposed by the rules. In this regard, the proponent must remember that the report has to be timely and complete; the report has to be primarily the work of the expert herself; and the report and expert interrogatory responses must be properly supplemented and corrected as information or analysis changes.

G.10. Expert reports supporting the case-in-chief and defense-in-chief are due 90 days before trial or the date set for trial, unless otherwise directed by the court, Fed. R. Civ. P. 26(a)(2)(C); rebuttal expert reports are due 30 days after receipt of the report which they rebut (Fed. R. Civ. P. 26(a)(2)(C)).

In terms of its authorship and content, the rebuttal report must comply with the rules covering initial reports. Attempts by counsel to introduce new theories or approaches, and new methodologies or new data through rebuttal reports, when those matters should properly have been part of the initial reports, should properly be rejected by the court. (See, also, Section C.7.)

H. Direct Examination of an Expert

H.1. Introduce the expert to the jury and the court.

"Dr. Smith, would you tell us your full name and your occupation?" Do not ask the witness to state her name "for the record," because everything goes into the record if it is supposed to, and besides that is not how people (as opposed to lawyers) talk.

H.2. Let the jury and judge know why the expert is there and should be listened to.

"Dr. Smith, have you come to court today prepared to state your expert opinion as to the effect on the environment of the spill of crude oil from the Amoco Cadiz when it was grounded in McMurdo Sound?" The witness should be explicitly told that she is not to answer this question by stating her opinion, but only by saying, "Yes, I have." The legal foundation for the opinion has not yet been laid, and in any event the jury is not ready to hear it, since they have not yet developed any confidence that the witness is credible. This is a tickler, intended to make the jury pay attention through the credentials which follow.

H.3. Invite your expert to first explain what qualifies them to give an opinion on the topic of this case.

For example, you would ask, "Dr. Smith, what qualifies you to give an opinion in this case?" Prepare your expert to respond by summarizing her strongest qualifications. For example, Dr. Smith might say, "I am qualified based on my extensive education concerning oil spills and their effect on the environment. I was personally responsible for overseeing the clean up of oil spilled in Alaska last year, and because of my observations, study, and research on the effects of this spill on the French coastline."

Then, continue the process of presenting credentials, emphasizing the connection between the work done in this case and the credentials being described. By "tailoring" the qualifications to this case, not only will you keep the jury interested (and the judge from rushing you by suggesting either a stipulation or a submission of resumes and leaving it at that), but you will help the witness describe more precisely what from her experience prepares her to give her opinion in this case. For example, you would ask, "Dr. Smith, have you taken any courses in college or graduate school that relate to the calculation of the dissolution of heavy crude oil in salt water?" This way, the jury or judge can see the relevance of the witness's education, training, and experience to an issue that they will have to deal with. In other words, these credentials can be seen as demonstrating the *helpfulness* of this witness, as required by Fed. R. Evid. 702.

H.4. Once the credentials have been presented as fully as the court, time, and the jury's patience allow, make a formal tender, if you are allowed.

A formal tender sounds like this: "Your Honor, plaintiff now tenders Dr. Mary Richards Smith to the Court as an expert in the field of marine biology, specializing in the impact on salt water environments, both animal and plant, of spills of crude oils and related hydrocarbons. She is qualified by reason of her experience, training, and education to provide opinion testimony on the subject of the long-term environmental effect of the spill which occurred from the Amoco Cadiz." Some jurisdictions no longer allow counsel to make a formal tender of an expert witness, because the court does not want the jury to think that the court is somehow sponsoring the witness's testimony. This is a mistake, because the court *is* sponsoring the testimony, at least to the extent of pointing out that because of her credentials, this witness is being authorized to provide her opinions which the jurors can consider like other evidence. Where the tender is permitted, it should be done. It signals the jury that something different is about to happen and it cues the judge that the credentials are finished and their adequacy to support the tendered testimony can be evaluated. After the tender is made, opposing counsel can request and conduct *voir dire*, if he chooses, seeking to demonstrate through questioning of the witness that there is an insufficient basis for allowing the opinion testimony. (*Voir dire* can also be requested during the direct examination of an expert on the substantive opinions, if the cross-examiner believes that the credentials are inadequate as a foundation for particular testimony, or that the opinions have gone beyond the areas of demonstrated expertise.)

H.5. Ask the expert for the major opinion.

This question should parallel the question in the tickler: "Dr. Smith, you have told us that you are prepared to state your expert opinion, that you hold with a reasonable degree of certainty in the field of marine biology, as to the effect on the environment of the spill of crude oil from the Amoco Cadiz in McMurdo Sound. What is that opinion?" The formality of the question calls attention to it, and the two-part form (introduction and question) helps assure that the jury and judge are listening so that they understand that you are getting to the important testimony. After this opinion is given by the witness, go through the other opinions that the expert has formed on major topics before you present the bases for any of those opinions. Find a way to illustrate the opinions visually, either using computer projection, magnetic cards, a whiteboard, or simply a pad on an easel. If the expert is permitted to come down from the stand and use the whiteboard, pad, or computer projector, it puts her into the professional mode and makes her more comfortable and the jury more attentive. Magnetic cards work especially well as props for counsel, so that you can peel off the card that says, "Generations of seals killed," and carry it with you while you question the witness on that topic. The jury will then have no doubt of the relevance of the questioning, because they will read the card every time they look at you.

H.6. Ask for the bases for the opinions, one by one, after all major opinions are out.

Under Fed. R. Evid. 705, the bases for an expert's opinions need not be disclosed on direct examination, although they must be disclosed if the expert is asked about them on cross-examination. Nevertheless, opinions without bases are not very persuasive. Therefore, after you have all of the important opinions out in front of the jury (and perhaps on the magnetic board or whiteboard or computer display), go back to the first opinion and ask the expert witness, "What is your basis for this opinion that thirty generations of seals will be affected by the spill of oil?" Follow-up questions are exactly those used at the deposition of the opposing expert to learn the details of his analysis: *What did you do? How did you do that? Why did you do that? What result did you get? What effect did that result have as you came to the opinion that thirty generations of seals would be affected?* Each time that you talk about the bases and their relationship to the conclusions or opinions, you can restate the opinion through the "looping" technique, in which the information to be emphasized is used as part of the follow-up question.

H.7. Anticipate and defuse cross-examination by asking about assumptions which the expert had to make.

All experts make assumptions; some assumptions are more explicit than others, but all experts make them. The assumptions may be trivial, like the assumption by the accident expert that whether the radio was turned on in the car was not relevant. Others may in fact be determinative of the outcome of the analysis, like the assumption by the forensic accountant that interest rates would remain low for the full thirty-year period of the future income stream that he is discounting to present value. Identify the significant assumptions made by your expert and present them during the direct examination, when the expert can justify them in a friendly and supportive atmosphere, rather than in the constricted and hostile environment of cross-examination. Ask the expert, "Did you have to make any assumptions in conducting your study of the ecology of McMurdo Sound? What were those assumptions? Why did you make that particular assumption? What effect would it have on your opinion if that assumption was varied by 10 percent?" Of course, this "sensitivity" questioning explores only those alternative assumptions within a range considered reasonable by your expert, who is prepared to state why the assumption she chose is the most reasonable of all (because it was in the middle of the range; because it had the most support in the scientific literature; because it comported with actual experience with this problem in other cases, etc.).

H.8. On re-direct examination, finish by allowing the witness to restate her main opinion.

After all cross-examination has finished, ask the witness, "Dr. Smith, on cross-examination we have heard questions about the degree of salinity of McMurdo Sound, and about the peculiar mating habits of McMurdo seals. There has also been questioning about other, much less severe, oil spills, and the ability of the seals in the Sound to survive. Had you considered that information before you formed your opinions in this matter? Having heard all of the information during the cross-examination, what is your opinion now as to the impact of the oil spill from the Amoco Cadiz on the reproductive capacity of the seal population in McMurdo Sound?" There we are then repeating the main point as the expert's exit line. (If there is re-cross-examination, attempting to raise another point, simply take that additional point and ask in re-re-direct, "Having considered the point raised by the owners of the Amoco Cadiz that wave action may have dispersed the oil within mere months, what is your opinion about the affect on the seals of this oil spill?")

H.9. For each main opinion, try to have one visual aid which makes a single, important point.

If you have an accounting case, then start with an exhibit that summarizes the simple calculation that the expert made in the case. For example, it might show total sales (956 million) minus all costs of goods sold and expenses (625 million) equals net profits (331 million). In addition, you may have worksheets and profit and loss statements which present twenty rows and seven columns of numbers, with net profit for the period being the single number in the lower right hand corner. If net profit is your point, then present, through the expert forensic accountant, a visual aid which shows only one number, "Net Profit = $7,459,372 for 1998."

Perhaps there is text, using words to describe how one got to net profit (total sales – returns – cost of goods sold – sales expenses – administrative expenses – taxes paid = net profit). The expert obviously knows what those other numbers are, but none of them is important to the jury. Therefore, emphasize the major point in an area of testimony by isolating it visually.

H.10. Supporting the expert.

Remember that you are selling the expert's credibility. If the jury or judge believes the expert even if they do not understand her, then they will accept her opinions and conclusions. Therefore, do not undermine the expert's credibility accidentally. If the expert slips and uses technical language, do not say, "Whoa, Doc, now, you've lost us there. Can you tell us common folk what 'epidemiology' means?" Just say, "Doctor, what is epidemiology?" You will be seen as supportive and polite, and the witness will be seen as knowledgeable. If the expert discusses matters out of order, do not say, "Wait a moment, now, Dr. Smith, I don't think that we are ready to talk about macrobiotics." Instead say, "Dr. Smith, is it necessary that we understand macrobiotics before we talk about the coastal ecosystem?"

I. Constructive Cross-Examination of an Expert

I.1. Constructive cross-examination must precede destructive cross-examination.

The suggestion to start on areas of agreement is based on the theory that once you antagonize the witness you will never get agreement from the witness. Some would argue that by making the witness mad, he or she will fight you even on the most obvious facts, and end up looking ridiculous. Others would say that starting with your best punch is necessary under principles of primacy (that the jury will remember best what they hear first). However, remember that the expert has some real advantages that other witnesses do not. Experts can hide behind jargon in their area of expertise. (Cross-examining is like pig wrestling, "both of you will get dirty, but only one of you will like it." Therefore, it is best to wrestle for as short a time as possible.)

The second reason to put constructive cross-examination before destructive cross-examination is that it makes better sense to the jury. Remember, destructive cross-examination challenges the witness's credibility; constructive cross-examination asks her to establish some points that you need or want. It makes little sense to say, in effect, "You are not to be believed, but I would like you to establish a few important things for me." It makes much more sense to extract your additional points constructively, and then to challenge the expert's credibility as it applies to the remainder of his assertions on direct examination.

I.2. Identify the areas in which the opposing parties' experts agree and establish through cross-examination that the opposing expert agrees with your expert.

You might use this technique to "enlist" the opposing expert's agreement that your expert has equal to or greater qualifications in the same or different areas than the expert. For example, some physicians will concede that the opposing expert shares hospital privileges with them, belongs to the same professional associations, or is board certified in areas where he or she is not.

In the typical, "battle of the experts" case, the opposing experts will agree on most of the facts in the case; after all, as experts in the same field, they have much more in common than they have in dispute. For example, they believe that the field of microeconomics has something to contribute to resolving the dispute; they believe that census data on the size and distribution of sizes of firms in an industry is appropriately studied; they agree that some data provides "snapshots" of the *status quo* at a single point in time, while time series data may show trends over time; they believe that conduct in an industry may alter structure, and that structure may alter conduct. Where they disagree may be on the single question of whether preventing a 10 percent increase in concentration by forbidding this merger will result in the maintenance of lower prices during the next five years — a very narrow question.

If the opposing expert is better credentialed than yours, force her on cross-examination to admit that she agrees with almost everything that your expert has done, from selection of sources through evaluation and presentation; number the items as you detail them, making an impressively long list of agreement, and then put the disagreement at the end, as one last number. That makes it look like 1 out of 17 points, a disagreement of only 6 percent, and leaves to the proponent of the witness the task of trying to explain that one point is, in reality, of overwhelming importance, equivalent to 60 percent, not 6 percent. The response to this (or the examination anticipating this) would instead categorize the points, perhaps into two groups — those affecting the firms' ability to earn monopoly profits, and those merely describing the market environment without affecting it. Then, the profit-related group is identified as being the locus of disagreement, so that it appears that the differences between the experts actually infect half of their work — the most important half.

I.3. The foundation for learned treatises can be established constructively.

Taking an approach similar to that you used during the deposition to encourage the opposing expert to identify learned treatises, you can ask on cross-examination, "Professor, you have spent considerable time reading the work of other researchers in your field, haven't you? And you have been able to identify some whose work is more reliable or useful than others, right? Those are the authors that you recommend to your graduate students for outside reading, or that you rely upon yourself as you write your books and papers for publication? One of those authorities is Professor John Smith, who wrote *The Economics of Early Puritan Settlements*, isn't that right?" Then tell the witness that you are going to read a paragraph from page 343 which relates to some point that she has made against your client during direct examination. Read the quote, and ask the witness whether you have read it correctly. Show her the text so that she can confirm your accurate reading. Do not ask whether she agrees; Fed. R. Evid. 803(18) does not require her to agree; it only requires you to call her attention to the quote. Notice that nothing in this constructive examination challenges the witnesses competence or credibility; she should be willing to admit that she tries to stay up with the literature in her field, and that she selects reliable materials to recommend to her students. Indeed, she could hardly claim otherwise. As a result, you have a very low-risk piece of cross-examination, always assuming that there is something in the learned treatise that contradicts the opposing expert and also makes sense to the judge and jury.

I.4. Avoid confrontation and accept whatever little or much the expert will give during this phase.

Confrontation does not serve your purposes during this "constructive" phase.

I.5. Preface questions with laudatory phrases, spoken without sarcasm, such as, "As an expert is this area, you would agree that. . . ."

Such language softens the tone and blunts the point on questions seeking agreement.

I.6. Do not challenge opinions during constructive cross-examination.

Instead, agree on sources, procedures, alternatives, necessary credentials, superior bases, and other matters not disputed between the experts.

I.7. Specifically present the data and other bases utilized by your expert and ask the opposing expert to agree that they are appropriately and

often relied upon by experts in the field (although perhaps not by him in this matter).

I.8. Establish the limitations imposed upon the expert witness by the demands of litigation.

Assumptions must be made to conserve time or supply the unknowable. Some projects must be left undone or un-begun. One often has to rely on lawyers to supply information. Predictions, especially about the future, can be difficult.

I.9. Ask the expert to agree to a statement narrowing the disagreement between him and your expert.

For example, "Then you would agree that you both use the same basic data, in basically the same way, but your approach assumes that future inflation will be considerably greater?"

I.10. Reserve impeachment for your "destructive" phase.

If the opposing expert does not wish to agree to, or concede, a point during this portion of the cross-examination, then reserve it for destructive cross-examination later if you have the controlling or impeaching materials. Do not destroy your further opportunities for constructive cross-examination by forgetting where you are in the structure of the examination.

J. Destructive Cross-Examination of an Expert

J.1. Do not let the opposing expert leave the witness chair to provide drawings, charts, graphs, sketches, lectures, or outlines by way of explanation.

The expert may be a very competent teacher, very comfortable in front of an audience. You have taken advantage of that during the deposition to encourage her to explain her work to you (see F.10, above); and her counsel has taken advantage of that teaching skill during direct examination. Now, on cross-examination, keep the witness in her chair, away from the whiteboard, the blackboard, the slide projector, and the posterboard exhibits. Make her sit and answer questions. You do not want to give her another opportunity to be interesting and persuasive; you want the jury to focus on *your* words, to be persuaded by what *you* say. Additionally, the expert may grow frustrated at not being able to stand up in front of the audience and lecture; good. If, after you have made your points, the expert asks for such an opportunity to come down and explain further ("Counsel, if I could just come down and show you a couple charts, I am certain that I could explain this point"), you might say something like, "Professor, let me just ask a couple more questions here, and perhaps we can handle this without spending too much time on it," or, "Well, I am going to move to something else here, Professor, but perhaps we'll have a chance to come back to that later."

J.2. Keep all questions tightly closed and short, so that there is no reasonable excuse for the expert to ask, "May I explain?"

When a reasonably complex question is asked, the judge might allow the expert to provide an explanation beyond just the "yes" or "no" answer you have sought. That appears fair, and you really cannot oppose an explanation in those circumstances without looking like you are trying to hide something from the jury. However, if your question is patently fair, and short, and clear, and can apparently be answered fully with a simple yes or no, then the expert's attempt to explain may seem like evasion. If the specific point is not crucial, graciously allow the explanation, and then ask the expert to give you the yes or no answer that your question called for. If the expert attempts this tactic in response to fair and clear leading questions, the jury will see it for the ruse that it is.

J.3. Begin with some unexpected topic, of moderate import, on which you have absolutely controlling material, such as deposition testimony.

This establishes the tone of the examination and you as the master. Or, begin with an analogy which you have tested with your expert that helps the jury understand your major disagreement. For example, in a wrongful death case where an economist is projecting damages over a twenty-year period, you might start by asking, "Do you play golf?" or "Have you ever watched golf on TV?" Then, "Isn't it true that on a long putt, if you are off just a little at the start, your ball can end up a long way from the hole?"

J.4. Save a high-interest, absolutely controlled point for the last line in the examination.

If all goes well through the rest of the examination, ask for a moment, review your notes, talk to your second chair, and then return to complete the examination on the high and successful point which you have reserved.

J.5. Sandwich chancier points in the middle, so that there will be no noticeable gaps if you abandon them uncompleted.

J.6. Use seven smaller questions, instead of one conclusory question, to make a point so that the judge and jury have sufficient time and information to appreciate what you are teaching them.

For example, knowing from report or deposition that the witness had not talked to the doctor who performed the autopsy, you could ask, "Dr.

Smithburn, you never spoke to the doctor who conducted the autopsy, did you?" Point made, but perhaps not appreciated. Instead ask, "Dr. Smithburn, I presume that you spent a number of hours, perhaps three or four, discussing the autopsy with the physician who performed it, is that correct?" "Well, at least you spent an hour or so with her, didn't you?" "Did you spend some time, then, on the telephone with that doctor, discussing the autopsy?" "Are you saying that you spent no time at all with the doctor who actually determined the cause of death?" "Did the lawyers tell you not to talk to that doctor, or was it your own idea?" This is especially effective with omissions and work not completed.

J.7. Emphasize facts which the expert has not utilized in her analysis and opinion.

If these facts are unknown to the expert, so much the better. This emphasis can come from repetition (create a list of facts not mentioned and re-read the entire list with each addition), "looping" the fact into the next question ("Did you decide not to talk to the autopsy doctor?" "After you decided not to talk to the autopsy doctor, did you examine tissue specimens yourself?"), or creating a visual record with a whiteboard, magnetic cards, an overhead projector, or even a blackboard.

J.8. Resist the instinct for the capillary.

Merely because you can impeach the witness does not mean that you should. Your capital with the judge and jury will be spent before your important points are made if you cannot resist the quibble or the niggle.

J.9. Impeach crisply and cleanly and then move on.

The significance of the change in testimony or position will be made apparent at closing argument.

J.10. Remember principles of high school science to help you determine your destructive theory.

It will help you keep the jury with you and understand the points you are making. For example, was your opponent biased, violating the principle that every scientist must guard his objectivity and not prejudge the results? Did the opposing expert fail to control all the important variables in the study he conducted? Did he reach his conclusion without considering all important data?

K. Experts, Summary Exhibits, Visual Aids, and Demonstrations

K.1. Use visual aids, charts, and graphs to provide the jury and judge with a picture story of the expert witness's testimony.

Although the expert's report may be hearsay (often admitted, but hearsay nevertheless), the conclusions in it and the support for those conclusions can often be presented to the court or jury in a memorable way through the use of colorful visual exhibits. Such exhibits probably need to be included in the expert's report, pursuant to Fed. R. Civ. P. 26(a)(2)(B), but this requirement may not be enforced by every judge in every federal court. Summary exhibits, under Fed. R. Evid. 1006, are admissible as convenient alternatives to voluminous writings and other materials. The expert's charts and graphs fit neatly into this definition. However, do not merely "blow up" the accountant's worksheet (with its columns and rows of numbers), or the engineer's spreadsheets of data points and curves. Create new visual exhibits, designed to be seen and not read — exhibits, in other words, which have impact immediately and visually. Non-summary exhibits can also be created and used to illustrate testimony, that is, to provide visual explanation of the expert's words from the stand. Fed. R. Evid. 803(17) allows the introduction, over hearsay objections, of excerpts from relevant market reports or commercial publications which the expert uses in her testimony, and learned treatise material under Fed. R. Evid. 803(18) might be presented to the expert on cross-examination using an attractive visual that has substantial impact. Remember, blowing textual documents up to two feet by three feet just gives you BIG textual documents. Visual exhibits — graphics — are pictures, not big words. Find a way to give the judge or jury a picture of your case and your expert's opinions.

K.2. Examine the opponent's visual exhibits (and your own) for "visual tricks."

When quantitative information is being displayed, such as price movements, volume changes, or market share increases, watch for subtle but misleading tricks, such as showing the baseline as something other than zero: a change from $8.00 for $9.00 looks much larger if the baseline is $7.00 rather than $0.00. A classic trick is to show changes with little icons, like oil barrels for increased petroleum imports, and then indicating a doubling of imports by doubling both the height and width of the icon, which of course increases the area (and impact) of the little barrel by a factor of four, not two. Your own graphic expert can help identify these misleading techniques for you. Yale Professor Edward Tufte has done the hard thinking on these topics in his three books, which are required reading for anyone attempting to use graphics to convey information. Professor Tufte especially warns against displaying one chart, then replacing it with another for a subsequent time period, and so on. Audiences cannot see change easily unless the different information is arrayed side by side, to permit easy comparison. Tufte calls the difficult, sequential display a problem of "One damn thing after another."

K.3. Rehearse the expert in working with and explaining the visual exhibits that have been prepared to accompany her testimony.

The expert should know the source of each data point, quotation, historical reference, or patient entry which appears on the visual exhibits. It is perfectly permissible for the expert to have her own copy of the exhibit in 8 ½ by 11" size, with annotations guiding her to the sources, and a key guiding her to the meaning of all of the symbols, so long as you remember that the opposition will be allowed to see the expert's version, on request.

K.4. In videotaped depositions to preserve expert testimony, have your expert use the actual visual exhibits, and then splice in close-ups of those exhibits when you present the tape at trial, while you place the actual exhibit in front of the jury, next to the screen or television.

This mixed-media presentation of the exhibits which the expert is using in the deposition gives them more reality, and allows the jury to follow the deposition testimony. After the testimony is over, provide the jurors with individual copies of the visual exhibits; if you do it during the testimony, then they may be looking at the exhibits instead of listening to the expert witness. The courtroom board showing the exhibit can be moved around, used with other witnesses, and left on the easel during other parts of your case, to give them more substance and reality in the judge's and jurors' minds.

K.5. On cross-examination, use at least one of the opposing expert's graphic exhibits against her own position.

For example, bring back an exhibit which the expert has used in her direct examination testimony, briefly remind the jury and judge how the exhibit was used, and then use it to illustrate alternative assumptions, additional facts, or errors in calculation or computation. You could cover the exhibit with a sheet of acetate and then ask the expert to mark certain challenged, erroneous, or questionable information by circling it on the acetate with a red marker. (Use acetate because it is not your exhibit to mark up, and, if it is in evidence, it would be impermissible to mark on it.) Those red circles will not be forgotten when the exhibit (and the acetate, with its own number) is reviewed in the jury room.

K.6. Include the expert in site photographs or videotapes of demonstrations and views.

Such photographic evidence not only shows the jury what the site looks like, or how the test or experiment was done (crash tests, accident reconstructions, product experiments), but it also shows that the expert was right there, sleeves rolled up, involved in the gathering of genuine, honest-to-goodness evidence that you cannot find in a classroom or library. Such credibility enhancement is so valuable that you should actively look for these opportunities to involve your expert. (Remember, however, that some of us, like Michael Dukakis, look silly when we put on helmets and climb into tanks.) (See B.11, above, for the use of this photographic opportunity technique to emphasize the expert's familiarity with the documentary evidence.)

K.7. Do not conduct live demonstrations in the courtroom.

There is something about the atmosphere of the courtroom (superheated air from extended debate, electrical currents from high tension, or burning rubber from great minds skidding before crashing) which prevents the normal rules of physics and nature from working properly. That is why projector light bulbs always burn out, computer programs always crash, VCRs are never correctly hooked up, and in-court demonstrations never work like they did in the laboratory three times the day before. Although they may not have the drama of live presentations, it is much safer to conduct your demonstrations in the lab and on videotape. If a lab demonstration does not work and it has to be shot on videotape again, then tell the judge and jury that up front, and explain why it did not work. At least the demonstration that they saw did work, and they will remember your successful run.

K.8. Visual or demonstrative evidence may be substantive evidence at the same time.

Illustrative evidence is offered solely to illustrate the witness's testimony; hence, the name. Evidence which has an evidentiary life of its own, separate from a witness's testimony, is substantive to that extent, and it may be offered as a separate basis for findings. As an example, a videotape from a police cruiser showing a high-speed chase and subsequent roadside arrest, may be offered to illustrate the arresting officer's testimony, as might a videotape of a re-enactment. The actual videotape could also be offered as substantive evidence of what actually occurred, independent from the testimony, and the jury could rely on the tape alone to find police abuse or resistance to lawful arrest. The re-enactment tape, however, is part and parcel of the testimony, and adds nothing substantive; indeed, if the testimony is stricken for some reason, then the illustrative re-enactment tape would also be stricken.

Demonstrative evidence is introduced to show how something happened, and it is substantive, not illustrative. Thus, if the witness comes down from the stand and "demonstrates" how the drunken customer walked out of the bar, after having told about it, the jury can base findings on the demonstration, regardless of the contents of the testimony. The demonstrative evidence has "independent substantive significance." When an acid and a base combine violently in a beaker, just as the expert testified that they would, the testimony has substantive significance, and the demonstration has substantive significance also, independent of the testimony of the expert. Demonstrative evidence adds to the testimony; illustrative testimony helps clarify the testimony, but the meaning resides in the testimony, not in the illustration of it.

K.9. Do not allow the opposing expert to use visuals during your cross-examination.

If the expert says, "I could explain that if you let me show you a few of my charts," then move on. Politely say, "We'll come back to that later if we have time, but I want to settle another point first." Or, you choose the exhibit to look at — one that you have cross-examination points on. But, do not allow the expert, on your cross-examination, to get back into her teaching mode, and to do it effectively with visual aids.

K.10. Because visual presentations are so important for persuasion and retention of information, ask potential experts to show you samples of visual exhibits from prior testimony.

Make visual facility as important as verbal ability in selecting your experts; after all, both are essential to presenting a persuasive and interesting view of the case. There are people (dubbed "left-brained" in pop psychological terms) who want to see footnotes and columns of numbers which add to 100 percent, and who are capable of absorbing information provided in non-graphic, textual formats, so long as it is logically presented and "vertically" arranged (that is, contains no intuitive or other "leaps" which are perceived as logical discontinuities by left-brained people); but there are also people, "right-brained" people, who want and perhaps need to see "pictures" in order to understand and remember a story. (In reality, it seems that most people have some of both right and left characteristics, and no one is all one or the other.) Make certain that you are presenting your expert case with enough "pictures" so that you reach all segments of the judge/jury audience and entertain and persuade them all.

L. Expert Depositions

There are two principal topics which must be discovered through the deposition of an expert or other discovery: first, what opinions has the expert come to, and, second, what are the bases for those opinions; that is, what methodology and data were used to develop those opinions? With the increased focus on the reliability of expert opinions brought to bear by the *Daubert* case and its progeny, examination on the subject of the methodology must cover not only how the opinion was developed, but what evidence there is that following such a methodology will likely result in reliable information.

For example, prior to *Daubert*, an expert might herself demonstrate the admissibility of her methodology by testifying that the approach had achieved general acceptance in the relevant scientific field, the old *Frye* test. We would inquire at deposition about the methodology and about her belief that it was generally accepted, but if she persisted in that testimony at trial, then the court would likely accept her opinions into the record. This is the *ipse dixit* approach criticized by the United States Supreme Court in *Daubert*: just because the expert says it is reliable, or accepted, does not make it so, and external evidence should be presented and examined.

By *Daubert*, a greater burden was placed upon the proponent of the expert testimony, thereby providing greater opportunities for challenge by the opponent, and those opportunities must be identified in the expert deposition. Now we look to see, for example, not only whether the expert believes that the methodology is generally accepted (because a modified *Frye* standard is one of the criteria recommended by *Daubert*), but we look for other evidence, beyond her testimony, that the field recognizes the methodology. Treatment of other criteria of reliability, including publication in peer-reviewed journals, known error rate, and testability and falsifiability, follows this same approach — we look beyond the expert's *ipse dixit* ("Yes, I believe that the error rate is acceptable").

In the following article, reprinted by permission of the authors, a number of criteria of reliability are examined, and for each a number of deposition questions are proposed, so that counsel can probe beyond the expert witness's *ipse dixit*. Of course, the Supreme Court has reminded us that the criteria for ascertaining reliability are as infinite as the fields of human knowledge, so there should be no mistake that these topics and questions are offered as exhaustive. Instead, they are offered as a starting point for thought about the question, "How do we know when someone else actually knows something?" and the even more difficult question, "How do we know when we know something?"

The Daubert Deposition Dance:

Retracing the Intricacies of the Expert's Steps

By David M. Malone and Ryan M. Malone

After the decision in *Daubert v. Merrill Dow*,[1] there was some question about whether the gatekeeping responsibilities of the federal trial courts extended to all expert testimony, or merely to "scientific" expert testimony. Even among circuits that believed that only scientific testimony was covered, there was confusion as to what was scientific testimony and what was "technical or other specialized" testimony. The *Kumho Tire*[2] case resolved that confusion, by clearly stating that the methodologies underlying *all* expert testimony must be evaluated for reliability.

This decision therefore clarified the occasions for application of the *Daubert* approach, although it compounded any remaining problems by increasing the number of cases covered. Chief among those remaining problems is the need for trial practitioners and trial courts to develop a coherent body of analytic tools by which methodological reliability can be measured with some confidence by lawyers and judges without formal training in the specialized fields. For example, how does the trial judge assess the reliability of methodologies employed by the astrophysicist, since it is unlikely that the trial judge coincidentally has been trained in astrophysics.[3]

Although the Supreme Court in *Daubert* and again in *Kumho Tire* emphasized that the four criteria — publication in a peer-reviewed journal; known or knowable error rate; general acceptance in the relevant scientific community; and testability or replicability (including the concept of "falsifiability"[4]) — were not exclusive (indeed, none of the four is even required), there seems to be some belief among attorneys and judges that we must measure reliability by those criteria alone. In an earlier article,[5] the authors suggested a number of additional, objective criteria that could be utilized in conducting this analysis, beyond those four mentioned in *Daubert*. Abstract criteria, whether four or fourteen, are not easily applied in discovery depositions, however, and we must recognize that it is in deposition that the foundation for challenge to an expert's methodology is uncovered. We therefore thought it might be useful to examine some specific questions that an attorney can ask at deposition to explore these various concepts of reliability, with follow-up and rationale explained as we go along.

1. *Publication in a peer-reviewed journal:* This criterion of reliability actually has two prongs to it: an article describing the methodology must have been published, which subjects it to scrutiny by whatever readership the journal has; and the article must have been reviewed, pre-publication, by "peers" in the particular field of knowledge, who ostensibly would scrutinize it for errors and challenge any unsupported conclusions. It is objective because it does not require the application of judgment to determine whether it has been satisfied; only examination of the literature. Deposition questions that examine whether this criterion has been satisfied are rather easy to create, but the exercise is useful:

    a.   *Where has this methodology been published?*

    b.   *Who published it?*

    c.   *What is the process for pre-publication review?*

    d.   *What are the credentials of the reviewers (sometimes called "referees")?*

    e.   *What criticisms or suggestions did the reviewers make?*

    f.   *What changes were made as a result of those suggestions?*

    g.   *What other changes were made?*

    h.   *What comments were received post-publication?*

i.   What is known of the credentials of those persons providing comments?

j.   What changes in methodology were made as a result of those comments?

k.   Have you, or has anyone else, published additional articles on this methodology?

2.   Known or knowable error rate: This criterion requests the expert to provide information about the likelihood that the methodology will produce incorrect results. It does not establish a threshold of correctness for admissibility, but it is difficult to believe that a court would admit an expert's opinions after hearing *in limine* testimony that a methodology may produce wrong results half the time. In the world of commercial litigation, economists and financial analysts may be the experts most susceptible to challenge based on a failure to satisfy this criterion; in truth, are they able even to assess their error rates when they conclude that a particular market structure is more competitive than another?

a.   Identify studies that have calculated error rates for this methodology.

b.   Describe how you yourself would determine the error rate.

c.   What mechanisms are available for reducing or eliminating errors?

d. *Is there a particular aspect of the methodology (e.g., data collection, data input, interpretation of results) that is more likely to produce errors?*

e. *How would someone employing this methodology know that an error had occurred?*

f. *What types of errors can occur?*

g. *What effect would those errors have on the utility or correctness of your opinion?*

3. General acceptance in the relevant scientific community: This is the (previously) well-established *Frye*[6] test. The weakness of this test was not that it asked an irrelevant question — the question is indeed relevant — but rather that it depended upon the expert for an opinion on the reliability of the methodology, rather than seeking objective information. As a sole criterion, however, it also assumes that the court could identify the relevant scientific community. Today, with specialists within specialties within sub-areas within practice areas within medical board areas, as an example, the nests of Russian dolls prevent any court from knowing, on its own, whether this is a "relevant scientific community" or a sub-specialty that should be evaluated according to standards from a larger group, or merely a fringe group of radicals. Furthermore, while mechanical engineering methodology may quite reasonably be scrutinized by application of the standards of mechanical engineering, as it was in *Kumho* Tire, we are not so confident that aromatherapist methodology should be evaluated only by application of the standards of aromatherapists. There is a skepticism here that we recognize and believe to be appropriate, even while we understand that we must be able to distinguish it from mere bias or prejudice.

> a. What evidence is there that practitioners in your field generally accept this approach?
>
> b. How do you define your field?
>
> c. What other approaches are utilized in that field?
>
> d. What approach is utilized most often?
>
> e. What are the advantages and disadvantages of the main methodologies?
>
> f. Why did you choose to use this methodology?
>
> g. When was this methodology developed?
>
> h. What effect did introduction of this methodology have on the acceptance of other methodologies?

4. Testability or replicability: It is not sufficient for a researcher to state that she has discovered a relationship between certain effects and a purported cause. She must specify that relationship in a sufficiently specific way that other researchers can examine it for themselves. If their examinations corroborate her results, then the hypothesis may become accepted. With such corroboration, however, her hypothesis stands as no better than conjecture. For example, several years ago at the National Heart, Lung and Blood Institute, a researcher noted a statistically significant correlation between people who ate sandwiches for lunch and people who developed serious heart disease. The researcher spelled out his methodology in sufficient detail that other researchers could review his approaches and data; they discovered that sandwiches and heart disease were not directly related to each other, but each was instead related to hurried meal times, a characteristic of Type A personalities at high risk for heart disease because of multiple stress factors. The original researcher's problem of *multicolinearity* would not have been observed if the original hypothesis had not been stated with sufficient specificity to permit test and replication.

a.   *Step by step, how have you conducted your tests or examinations?*

b.   *Identify all of your data sources.*

c.   *Provide all of your laboratory or session notes.*

d. *Beginning with a particular item of raw (empirical) data, show us how it is treated or manipulated by the methodology.*

e. *What tests did you do yourself to confirm that the methodology produced parallel results for parallel inputs? (If your methodology is addition and you input [2, 2] and get 4, then when you input [4, 4] you should get 8.)*

f. *What tests did you do to confirm that disparate inputs would yield disparate results? (If the factor of few firms in an industry is said to lead to high profits, then we should not observe industries with many firms also enjoying high profits. For a simpler analogy, if a friend says that a black box will light a red light when salted pretzels are inserted, it is not a sufficient test to insert salted pretzels and watch for the light; we must also insert unsalted pretzels and stale GummiBear candies and watch for the light. Otherwise, we might merely have a machine (methodology) that turns on a light when anything is inserted.)*

5. **Development and use of the methodology in non-litigation contexts:** The Ninth Circuit, on remand in the *Daubert* matter, grafted an additional criterion onto the four suggested by the Supreme Court: Was the methodology developed

for non-litigation purposes?[7] Questioning on this criterion should be reasonably straightforward, because it asks the expert for historical facts, not scientific opinions or relationships. If the methodology was developed solely (or, logically, primarily) for the purpose of supporting a particular side in litigation, we are more skeptical about its objectivity.

    a.   *When was this methodology developed?*

    b.   *Who was the developer?*

    c.   *What was the original purpose of its development?*

    d.   *Are you using any modifications that were developed for litigation?*

    e.   *Why were modifications made to the original methodology?*

    f.   *Is the methodology still being used for its original purpose?*

    g.   *Has it been partially or largely supplanted?*

    h.   *What methodologies have supplanted it? Why?*

6.   Sufficiency to explain the salient facts: The Supreme Court in *Kumho Tire* expressed skepticism that a practitioner of a legitimate methodology ("visual and tactile tire failure analysis") could not evaluate whether an apparently salient fact was present (whether the tire had traveled

50,000 miles or more).[8] This does involve the *a priori* belief on the part of the Court that this factor is significant; nevertheless, the expert should at least have been able to provide a reasonable explanation for his inability to determine this fact.

a.   Describe all of the categories of information that were available to you for this analysis (or that are generated by the event being analyzed: profits, margins, gross sales revenue, industry concentration, firm rank, unit sales, advertising-to-sales ratios, advertising expenditure ramps, etc.).

b.   Rank those categories of data from most to least significant, and explain the ranking.

c.   Show us where each of those categories was used.

d.   Tell us why some categories of data were not used.

e.   Tell us how you adjusted for your inability to obtain some data (e.g., tire travel miles).

f.   Have you considered different data in other cases? Why?

g.   Do other researchers consider other data or rank the data differently in importance?

h.   Have you ever reached conclusions without data from each category?

7. Quantitative sufficiency of the data employed: In an industrial conveyor belt failure case,[9] the court was concerned that the mechanical engineer was relying on a very small sample to provide data points for his analysis: a few bolts from a very large conveyor assembly. While testimony from someone trained in statistical methods might satisfy the court that the data were sufficient for conclusions at a reasonable level of certainty, the mechanical engineer could not provide that foundation, and the court was uncomfortable with the minimal basis.

a. *What were your sources of data?*

b. *How much data was available from each source?*

c. *Was there richer data available elsewhere?*

d. *Was a statistical analysis performed to determine the adequacy of the data for the purpose of drawing conclusions?*

e. *At what confidence level did the data allow you to draw your conclusions?*

f. *At what confidence level do you typically operate in non-litigation activities in your profession?*

g. *In your last published article, what confidence level did you employ?*

h. *In the last article that you read or refereed, what confidence level was employed?*

i. *If the data points were increased by a factor of 2, how would the confidence level have been affected? If the points were increased tenfold?*

j. *If one-third of the data you used were determined to be unreliable, would your conclusions still be sound, at the same level of confidence?*

8. *Qualitative sufficiency of the data employed:* In some cases, we can imagine that the data are quantitatively sufficient (we have enough data points to satisfy the statisticians among us), but we are troubled by the quality of the data or its sources. For example, in child abuse cases, experts sometimes are willing to testify based in part upon their experiences with descriptions of abuse and its sequela from numerous children. The sample may be sufficient in size; even the simple hearsay nature of the bases may be so commonly encountered that it does not disqualify the testimony; but the impressionable nature of the sources — children interviewed under unknown and perhaps uncontrolled circumstances, having been subjected to unrevealed pressures or influences — renders them suspect and may impel a court to exclude the expert testimony.

a. What were the sources of your data?

b. Who collected the data?

c. Who supplied the data to the persons collecting it?

d. What prior experience have you had with this methodology for data collection?

e. What tests did you conduct to determine that your data were accurate?

f. What motivations were provided to the sources to encourage accurate reporting?

g. Were there any penalties for inaccurate reporting by the sources to your collectors?

h. What were the sources told about the purposes of the data collection?

i. What were the collectors told about the purposes?

j. What were the criteria for including and excluding sources of data?

9. Consistency with general methodology: Methodologies should be reliable regardless of the context-based biases or prejudices of the persons employing them. For example, the methodology the expert uses to determine the quality of structural steel should be the same, whether that examination is being done as quality control for an industry member, as consultant to a plaintiff in a contract suit, or as consultant to a defendant in a products liability suit. Of course, the general approach should be identified first at deposition, before questioning about specifics; otherwise, the description of what is generally done will be adjusted to match what the witness already said was done in this case. In *Kumho Tire* itself, the Court was interested in the fact that the expert said that his approach involved analysis of four "visual and tactile" aspects of the failed tire and, if any two were present, concluding that the failure was the result of owner abuse rather than manufacturing defect. The expert then found two factors to be present (apparently one just a little bit), but he nevertheless concluded that the failure resulted from defect. This departure from his general methodology may have been fatal to his opinion.[10]

a. *Tell me the steps in using this analysis in your everyday, non-litigation work.*

b. *What are the uses of such analysis?*

c. *What data do you obtain; from what sources?*

d. *Who assists you? Why? How?*

e. *When have you used this analysis before?*

f. *Did you follow the general methodology you have just described?*

g. *In this litigation, what steps do you perform in this analysis?*

h.   *Who assisted you? Why? How?*

i.   *Was it necessary to depart from the general approach in any way? Why?*

j.   *What precautions did you take to insure that those departures would not inappropriately affect the results of the analysis?*

k.   *What authority did you have for believing those precautions were sufficient?*

l.   *What other steps did you take that were different from your general approach or methodology?*

10. *Existence of a body of literature on the particular methodology:* If there is no body of literature on the methodology that the expert is recommending, and the explanation for such absence is not apparent or the expert cannot or does not explain the absence of such literature, then the court is justified in exercising skepticism about the reliability of the methodology. (Of course, other factors would be affected also, such as "general acceptance in the relevant scientific community;" how would such acceptance be evidenced if there is no literature?) Of course, if the field of expertise would not be expected to generate such a body of literature ("the adequacy of methods for cleaning tomato sauce spills in supermarket aisles"), the court might well ignore this factor. A faulty syllogism could lead people to believe that, because there is a body of literature on an approach, it represents a reliable methodology; it may merely mean that there are lots of unreliable adherents who write lots of unreliable stuff.[11] The field of astrology, as an example, has generated thousands of books and articles over centuries (or millennia, if Druidic runes qualify).

a. *How does one learn about this methodology?*

b. *How do you keep up with changes and improvements in the methodology?*

c. *What are the principal journals or publications in this field?*

d. *Who contributes to them?*

e. *Who referees or edits them for methodological correctness?*

f. *Do noted scientists contribute or subscribe? (E.g., do astronomers subscribe or contribute to the "Astrologers' Journal"?)*

g. *Do contributors or editors appear in journals of related and accepted fields? (E.g., do astrologers get published in the "American Journal of Astronomy"?)*

h. *How long have the main journals in the field been published?*

11. *Logical derivation of the methodology:* Experience suggests that the scientific progress is, indeed, progressive; that is, new developments build in some recognizable and articulable way on past, related explorations: blood-letting did not lead immediately to heart transplantations; green Post-It™ notes followed yellow Post-It™ notes; and the methods for putting a human on the moon depended upon the development of methods for putting a human in Earth orbit. As a general, *a priori* principle that makes us comfortable, few steps are skipped. When steps *are* skipped in such normally evolutionary change, so that it becomes revolutionary, we look for explanations, and we expect the proponent of the new theory to provide those explanations.

a. Describe the derivation of the methodology that you used.

b. What prior methodology is this one most closely related to?

c. Describe the similarities between them. Describe the differences.

d. What problems or factors led to the change from the old to the new methodology?

e. Who were the foremost proponents of the prior methodology?

f. Who initiated, sponsored, or championed the change to the new methodology?

g.   *What role did you have in this change?*

h.   *In what circumstances would the two meth-odologies yield different results?*

i.   *What specific differences in the methodologies lead to those different results?*

j.   *Why is the new methodology superior?*

Conclusion

The Supreme Court in *Kumho Tire* emphasized that it would be fruitless to attempt to list all crite-ria for assessing reliability of experts' methodolo-gies, because they are as numerous as the fields of human knowledge.[12] The purpose of this article is obviously not to disagree with the Court on this point, but rather to suggest ways of thinking about reliability, approaches to assessing meth-odologies, that can be used across fields of exper-tise, and that do not depend on requiring the lawyers or the judges to develop competence in the field being assessed. As we consider these le-gal questions (both the question of how to deter-mine reliability and the questions being suggested here as part of a solution), we are in fact considering questions of much broader appli-cation to the human condition: How do we learn? How do we know when we know? How can we learn what someone else *actually* knows? If we were concerned only with the question — trivial in this context — of determining the credibility of an expert, traditional tools are available: cross-examination, impeachment, learned treatises, omissions, and so forth. Instead, in considering *Daubert-Kumho Tire* issues, we must concern ourselves with the possibility of truth-telling witnesses, armed with patently impressive credentials, whose science may represent the future, but whose testimony should not be presented in court.

Endnotes

1. *See* Daubert v. Merrill Dow Pharmaceuticals, Inc., 509 U.S. 579 (1993).

2. *See* Kumho Tire Co. v. Carmichael, 526 U.S. 137 (1999).

3. Some suggest that the court could overcome this problem by obtaining its own expert (at the parties' expense, of course). This is not a solution, however, because the question of the reliability of expert methodologies would then legitimately be directed toward the court's expert and her methodologies. Pundits might suggest that another court-retained expert could be consulted, and then another, until we complete some regression back to a Prime Expert.

4. A premise is "falsifiable" if it can be proven wrong, usually through direct experience. For instance, the premise "all ravens are black" is falsifiable, since it can be proven wrong by the discovery of a white raven. On the other hand, the premise "everything in the universe doubles in size for a second, and then it halves in size the next second" is not falsifiable, since it is impossible to disprove through direct experience. (If everything is alternating in doubling and halving in size, it remains *relatively* the same size, and therefore the difference is impossible to measure.) Scientific premises are tentative and falsifiable, while some other premises are not. It is common for creationists to point out that evolutionary biologists often contradict parts of evolutionary theory. However, the testing of evolutionary theory by its subscribers, which the creationists see as a weakness of that theory, is actually proof positive that

the theory is scientific. *See, e.g.,* ROBERT T. PINNOCK, TOWER OF BABEL: THE EVIDENCE AGAINST THE NEW CREATIONISTS, xvi (MIT Press 2000): "Science imposes severe constraints upon itself to ensure that its conclusions are intersubjectively testable, constraints that require that it not appeal to supernatural hypotheses or allow the citation of special (private) revelations as evidence. The new creationists, including Johnson and philosophers such as Alvin Plantinga, reject these constraints and share the view that supernatural explanations should be admitted into science."

5. *See* David M. Malone & Ryan M. Malone, *The Zodiac Expert: Reliability After Kumho*, 22 THE TRIAL LAWYER MAGAZINE 265 (Fall 1999).

6. *See* Frye v. United States, 293 F. 1013 (D.C. Cir. 1923).

7. *See* Daubert v. Merrill Dow Pharmaceuticals, Inc., 43 F.3d 1311 (9th Cir. 1995).

8. *See* Kumho Tire, 526 U.S. at 254.

9. Watkins v. Telsmith, 121 F.3d 984 (5th Cir. 1997).

10. *See* Kumho Tire, 526 U.S. at 254–55.

11. In order to be certain that we can identify faulty syllogisms, let us look at a correct syllogism and a faulty syllogism:

- Correct syllogism A: (1) All frogs are green; (2) Clyde is a frog; therefore (3) Clyde is green.

- Correct syllogism B: (1) All frogs are green; (2) Clyde is not green; therefore (3) Clyde is not a frog.

- Incorrect syllogism C: (1) All frogs are green; (2) Clyde is green; therefore (3) Clyde is a frog. This is incorrect because Clyde could be something else that is green but not a frog, such as a pet lime.

Now, applying this syllogistic template to the *Daubert* methodology questions:

- Correct syllogism D: (1) Reliable methodologies are likely to generate relatively substantial literature; (2) this is a reliable methodology; therefore (3) it is likely to generate (or to have generated) a relatively substantial body of literature.

- Correct syllogism E: Reliable methodologies are likely to generate relatively substantial literature; (2) this methodology has not generated relatively substantial literature; therefore (3) this is not a reliable methodology (or, even more correctly, this *is not likely to be* a reliable methodology).

- Incorrect syllogism F: (1) Reliable methodologies are likely to generate relatively substantial literature; (2) this methodology has generated a relatively substantial body of literature; (3) therefore this is a reliable methodology.

12. *See* Kumho Tire, 526 U.S. at 251.

Federal Rules of Evidence

as amended to December 1, 2000

Rule 602 — Lack of Personal Knowledge

A witness may not testify to a matter unless evidence is introduced sufficient to support a finding that the witness has personal knowledge of the matter. Evidence to prove personal knowledge may, but need not, consist of the witness' own testimony. This rule is subject to the provisions of rule 703, relating to opinion testimony by expert witnesses.

Rule 604 — Interpreters

An interpreter is subject to the provisions of these rules relating to qualification as an expert and the administration of an oath or affirmation to make a true translation.

Rule 701 — Opinion Testimony by Lay Witnesses

If the witness is not testifying as an expert, the witness' testimony in the form of opinions or inferences is limited to those opinions or inferences which are (a) rationally based on the perception of the witness, (b) helpful to a clear understanding of the witness' testimony or the determination of a fact in issue, and (c) not based on scientific, technical, or other specialized knowledge within the scope of Rule 702.

Rule 702 — Testimony by Experts

If scientific, technical, or other specialized knowledge will assist the trier of fact to understand the evidence or to determine a fact in issue, a witness qualified as an expert by knowledge, skill, experience, training, or education, may testify thereto in the form of an opinion or otherwise, if (1) the testimony is based upon sufficient facts or data, (2) the testimony is the product of reliable principles and methods, and (3) the witness has applied the principles and methods reliably to the facts of the case.

Rule 703 — Bases of Opinion Testimony by Experts

The facts or data in the particular case upon which an expert bases an opinion or inference may be those perceived by or made known to the expert at or before the hearing. If of a type reasonably relied upon by experts in the particular field in forming opinions or inferences upon the subject, the facts or data need not be admissible in evidence in order for the opinion or inference to be admitted. Facts or data that are otherwise inadmissible shall not be disclosed to the jury by the proponent of the opinion or inference unless the court determines that their probative value in assisting the jury to evaluate the expert's opinion substantially outweighs their prejudicial effect.

Rule 704 — Opinion on Ultimate Issue

(a) Except as provided in subdivision (b), testimony in the form of an opinion or inference otherwise admissible is not objectionable because it embraces an ultimate issue to be decided by the trier of fact.

(b) No expert witness testifying with respect to the mental state or condition of a defendant in a criminal case may state an opinion or inference as to whether the defendant did or did not have the mental state or condition constituting an element of the crime charged or of a defense thereto. Such ultimate issues are matters for the trier of fact alone.

Rule 705 — Disclosure of Facts or Data Underlying Expert Opinion

The expert may testify in terms of opinion or inference and give reasons therefor without first testifying to the underlying facts or data, unless the court requires otherwise. The expert may in any event be required to disclose the underlying facts or data on cross-examination.

Rule 706 — Court Appointed Experts

(a) **Appointment.** The court may on its own motion or on the motion of any party enter an order to show cause why expert witnesses should not be appointed, and may request the parties to submit nominations. The court may appoint any expert witnesses agreed upon by the parties, and may appoint expert witnesses of its own selection. An expert witness shall not be appointed by the court unless the witness consents to act. A witness so appointed shall be informed of the witness' duties by the court in writing, a copy of which shall be filed with the clerk, or at a conference in which the parties shall have opportunity to participate. A witness so appointed shall advise the parties of the witness' findings, if any; the witness' deposition may be taken by any party; and the witness may be called to testify by the court or any party. The witness shall be subject to cross-examination by each party, including a party calling the witness.

(b) **Compensation.** Expert witnesses so appointed are entitled to reasonable compensation in whatever sum the court may allow. The compensation thus fixed is payable from funds which may be provided by law in criminal cases and civil actions and proceedings involving just compensation under the fifth amendment. In other civil actions and proceedings the compensation shall be paid by the parties in such proportion and at such time as the court directs, and thereafter charged in like manner as other costs.

(c) Disclosure of appointment. In the exercise of its discretion, the court may authorize disclosure to the jury of the fact that the court appointed the expert witness.

(d) Parties' experts of own selection. Nothing in this rule limits the parties in calling expert witnesses of their own selection.

Rule 803 — Hearsay Exceptions; Availability of Declarant Immaterial

The following are not excluded by the hearsay rule, even though the declarant is available as a witness:

. . .

(17) Market reports, commercial publications. Market quotations, tabulations, lists, directories, or other published compilations, generally used and relied upon by the public or by persons in particular occupations.

(18) Learned treatises. To the extent called to the attention of an expert witness upon cross-examination or relied upon by the expert witness in direct examination, statements contained in published treatises, periodicals, or pamphlets on a subject of history, medicine, or other science or art, established as a reliable authority by the testimony or admission of the witness or by other expert testimony or by judicial notice. If admitted, the statements may be read into evidence but may not be received as exhibits.

Rule 1006 — Summaries

The contents of voluminous writings, recordings, or photographs which cannot conveniently be examined in court may be presented in the form of a chart, summary, or calculation. The originals, or duplicates, shall be made available for examination or copying, or both, by other parties at reasonable time and place. The court may order that they be produced in court.

Federal Rules of Civil Procedure

as amended to December 1, 2000

Rule 26. General Provisions Governing Discovery; Duty of Disclosure

(a) Required Disclosures; Methods to Discover Additional Matter.

(1) Initial Disclosures. Except in categories of proceedings specified in Rule 26(a)(1)(E), or to the extent otherwise stipulated or directed by order, a party must, without awaiting a discovery request, provide to other parties:

(A) the name and, if known, the address and telephone number of each individual likely to have discoverable information that the disclosing party may use to support its claims or defenses, unless solely for impeachment, identifying the subjects of the information;

(B) a copy of, or a description by category and location of, all documents, data compilations, and tangible things that are in the possession, custody, or control of the party and that the disclosing party may use to support its claims or defenses, unless solely for impeachment;

(C) a computation of any category of damages claimed by the disclosing party, making available for inspection and copying as under Rule 34 the documents or other evidentiary material, not privileged or protected from disclosure, on which such computation is based, including materials bearing on the nature and extent of injuries suffered; and

(D) for inspection and copying as under Rule 34 any insurance agreement under which any person carrying on an insurance business may be liable to satisfy part or all of a judgment which may be entered in the action or to indemnify or reimburse for payments made to satisfy the judgment.

(E) The following categories of proceedings are exempt from initial disclosure under Rule 26(a)(1):

(i) an action for review on an administrative record;

(ii) a petition for habeas corpus or other proceeding to challenge a criminal conviction or sentence;

(iii) an action brought without counsel by a person in custody of the United States, a state, or a state subdivision;

(iv) an action to enforce or quash an administrative summons or subpoena;

(v) an action by the United States to recover benefit payments;

(vi) an action by the United States to collect on a student loan guaranteed by the United States;

(vii) a proceeding ancillary to proceedings in other courts; and

(viii) an action to enforce an arbitration award.

These disclosures must be made at or within 14 days after the Rule 26(f) conference unless a different time is set by stipulation or court order, or unless a party objects during the conference that initial disclosures are not appropriate in the circumstances of the action and states the objection in the Rules 26(f) discovery plan. In ruling on the objection, the court must determine what disclosures—if any—are to be made, and set the time for disclosure. Any party first served or otherwise joined after the Rules 26(f) conference must make these disclosures within 30 days after being served or joined unless a different time is set by stipulation or court order. A party must make its initial disclosures based on the information then reasonably available to it and is not excused from making its disclosures because it has not fully completed its investigation of the case or because it challenges the sufficiency of another party's disclosures or because another party has not made its disclosures.

(2) Disclosure of Expert Testimony.

(A) In addition to the disclosures required by paragraph (1), a party shall disclose to other parties the identity of any person who may be used at trial to present evidence under Rules 702, 703, or 705 of the Federal Rules of Evidence.

(B) Except as otherwise stipulated or directed by the court, this disclosure shall, with respect to a witness who is retained or specially employed to provide expert testimony in the case or whose duties as an employee of the party regularly involve giving expert testimony, be accompanied by a written report prepared and signed by the witness. The report shall contain a complete statement of all opinions to be expressed and the basis and reasons therefor; the data or other information considered by the witness in forming the opinions; any exhibits to be used as a summary of or support for the opinions; the qualifications of the witness, including a list of all publications authored by the witness within the preceding ten years; the compensation to be paid for the study and testimony; and a listing of any other cases in which the witness has testified as an expert at trial or by deposition within the preceding four years.

(C) These disclosures shall be made at the times and in the sequence directed by the court. In the absence of other directions from the court or stipulation by the parties, the disclosures shall be made at least 90 days before the trial date or the date the case is to be ready for trial or, if the evidence is intended solely to contradict or rebut evidence on the same subject matter identified by another party under paragraph (2)(B), within 30 days after the disclosure made by the other party. The parties shall supplement these disclosures when required under subdivision(e)(1).

(3) Pretrial Disclosures. In addition to the disclosures required by Rules 26(a)(1) and (2), a party must provide to other parties and promptly file with the court the following information regarding the evidence that it may present at trial other than solely for impeachment:

> **(A)** the name and, if not previously provided, the address and telephone number of each witness, separately identifying those whom the party expects to present and those whom the party may call if the need arises;

> **(B)** the designation of those witnesses whose testimony is expected to be presented by means of a deposition and, if not taken stenographically, a transcript of the pertinent portions of the deposition testimony; and

> **(C)** an appropriate identification of each document or other exhibit, including summaries of other evidence, separately identifying those which the party expects to offer and those which the party may offer if the need arises.

Unless otherwise directed by the court, these disclosures must be made at least 30 days before trial. Within 14 days thereafter, unless a different time is specified by the court, a party may serve and promptly file a list disclosing (i) any objections to the use under Rule 32(a) of a deposition designated by another party under Rule 26(a)(3)(B), and (ii) any objection, together with the grounds therefor, that may be made to the admissibility of materials identified under Rule 26(a)(3)(C). Objections not so disclosed, other than objections under Rules 402 and 403 of the Federal Rules of Evidence, are waived unless excused by the court for good cause.

(4) **Form of Disclosures.** Unless the court orders otherwise, all disclosures under Rule 26(a)(1) through (3) must be made in writing, signed, and served.

(5) **Methods to Discover Additional Matter.** Parties may obtain discovery by one or more of the following methods: depositions upon oral examination or written questions; written interrogatories; production of documents or things or permission to enter upon land or other property under Rule 34 or 45(a)(1)(C), for inspection and other purposes; physical and mental examinations; and requests for admission.

(b) **Discovery Scope and Limits.** Unless otherwise limited by order of the court in accordance with these rules, the scope of discovery is as follows:

(1) In General. Parties may obtain discovery regarding any matter, not privileged, which is relevant to the claim or defense of any party, including the existence, description, nature, custody, condition, and location of any books, documents, or other tangible things and the identity and location of persons having knowledge of any discoverable matter. For good cause, the court may order discovery of any matter relevant to the subject matter involved in the action. Relevant information need not be admissible at the trial if the discovery appears reasonably calculated to lead to the discovery of admissible evidence. All discovery is subject to the limitations imposed by Rule 26(b)(2)(i), (ii), and (iii).

(2) Limitations. By order, the court may alter the limits in these rules on the number of depositions and interrogatories or the length of depositions under Rule 30. By order or local rule, the court may also limit the number of request under Rule 36. The frequency or extent of use of the discovery methods otherwise permitted under these rules and by any local rule shall be limited by the court if it determines that: (i) the discovery sought is unreasonably cumulative or duplicative, or is obtainable from some other source that is more convenient, less burdensome, or less expensive; (ii) the party seeking discovery has had ample opportunity by discovery in the action to obtain the information sought; or (iii) the burden or expense of the proposed discovery outweighs its likely benefit, taking into account the needs of the case, the amount in controversy, the parties' resources, the importance of the issues at stake in the litigation, and the importance of the proposed discovery in resolving the issues. The court may act upon its own initiative after reasonable notice or pursuant to a motion under Rule 26(c).

(3) Trial Preparation: Materials. Subject to the provisions of subdivision (b)(4) of this rule, a party may obtain discovery of documents and tangible things otherwise discoverable under subdivision (b)(1) of this rule and prepared in anticipation of litigation or for trial by or for another party or by or for that other party's representative (including the other party's attorney, consultant, surety, indemnitor, insurer, or agent) only upon a showing that the party seeking discovery has substantial need of the materials in the preparation of the party's case and that the party is unable without undue hardship to obtain the substantial equivalent of the materials by other means. In ordering discovery of such materials when the required showing has been made, the court shall protect against disclosure of the mental impressions, conclusions, opinions, or legal theories of an attorney or other representative of a party concerning the litigation.

A party may obtain without the required showing a statement concerning the action or its subject matter previously made by that party. Upon request, a person not a party may obtain without the required showing a statement concerning the action or its subject matter previously made by that person. If the request is refused, the person may move for a court order. The provisions of Rule 37(a)(4) apply to the award of expenses incurred in relation to the motion. For purposes of this paragraph, a statement previously made is (A) a written statement signed or otherwise adopted or approved by the person making it, or (B) a stenographic, mechanical, electrical, or other recording, or a transcription thereof, which is a substantially verbatim recital of an oral statement by the person making it and contemporaneously recorded.

(4) Trial Preparation: Experts.

(A) A party may depose any person who has been identified as an expert whose opinions may be presented at trial. If a report from the expert is required under subdivision (a)(2)(B), the deposition shall not be conducted until after the report is provided.

(B) A party may, through interrogatories or by deposition, discover facts known or opinions held by an expert who has been retained or specially employed by another party in anticipation of litigation or preparation for trial and who is not expected to be called as a witness at trial only as provided in Rule 35(b) or upon a showing of exceptional circumstances under which it is impracticable for the party seeking discovery to obtain facts or opinions on the same subject by other means.

(C) Unless manifest injustice would result, (i) the court shall require that the party seeking discovery pay the expert a reasonable fee for time spent in responding to discovery under this subdivision; and (ii) with respect to discovery obtained under subdivision (b)(4)(B) of this rule the court shall require the party seeking discovery to pay the other party a fair portion of the fees and expenses reasonably incurred by the latter party in obtaining facts and opinions from the expert.

(5) Claims of Privilege or Protection of Trial Preparation Materials. When a party withholds information otherwise discoverable under these rules by claiming that it is privileged or subject to protection as trial preparation material, the party shall make the claim expressly and shall describe the nature of the documents, communications, or things not produced or disclosed in a manner that, without revealing information itself privileged or protected, will enable other parties to assess the applicability of the privilege or protection.

(c) Protective Orders. Upon motion by a party or by the person from whom discovery is sought, accompanied by a certification that the movant has in good faith conferred or attempted to confer with other affected parties in an effort to resolve the dispute without court action, and for good cause shown, the court in which the action is pending or alternatively, on matters relating to a deposition, the court in the district where the deposition is to be taken may make any order which justice requires to protect a party or person from annoyance, embarrassment, oppression, or undue burden or expense, including one or more of the following:

(1) that the disclosure or discovery not be had;

(2) that the disclosure or discovery may be had only on specified terms and conditions, including a designation of the time or place;

(3) that the discovery may be had only by a method of discovery other than that selected by the party seeking discovery;

(4) that certain matters not be inquired into, or that the scope of the disclosure or discovery be limited to certain matters;

(5) that discovery be conducted with no one present except persons designated by the court;

(6) that a deposition, after being sealed, be opened only by order of the court;

(7) that a trade secret or other confidential research, development, or commercial information not be revealed or be revealed only in a designated way; and

(8) that the parties simultaneously file specified documents or information enclosed in sealed envelopes to be opened as directed by the court.

If the motion for a protective order is denied in whole or in part, the court may, on such terms and conditions as are just, order that any party or other person provide or permit discovery. The provisions of Rule 37(a)(4) apply to the award of expenses incurred in relation to the motion.

(d) Timing and Sequence of Discovery. Except in categories of proceedings exempted from initial disclosure under Rule 26(a)(1)(E), or when authorized under these rules or by order or agreement of the parties, a party may not seek discovery from any source before the parties have conferred as required by Rule 26(f). Unless the court upon motion, for the convenience of parties and witnesses and in the interests of justice, orders otherwise, methods of discovery may be used in any sequence, and the fact that a party is conducting discovery, whether by deposition or otherwise, does not operate to delay any other party's discovery.

(e) Supplementation of Disclosures and Responses. A party who has made a disclosure under subdivision (a) or responded to a request for discovery with a disclosure or response is under a duty to supplement or correct the disclosure or response to include information thereafter acquired if ordered by the court or in the following circumstances:

> **(1)** A party is under a duty to supplement at appropriate intervals its disclosures under

subdivision (a) if the party learns that in some material respect the information disclosed is incomplete or incorrect and if the additional or corrective information has not otherwise been made known to the other parties during the discovery process or in writing. With respect to testimony of an expert from whom a report is required under subdivision (a)(2)(B) the duty extends both to information contained in the report and to information provided through a deposition of the expert, and any additions or other changes to this information shall be disclosed by the time the party's disclosures under Rule 26(a)(3) are due.

(2) A party is under a duty seasonably to amend a prior response to an interrogatory, request for production, or request for admission if the party learns that the response is in some material respect incomplete or incorrect and if the additional or corrective information has not otherwise been made known to the other parties during the discovery process or in writing.

(f) Conference of Parties; Planning for Discovery. Except in categories of proceedings exempted from initial disclosure under Rule 26(a)(1)(E) or when otherwise ordered, the parties must, as soon as practicable and in any event at least 21 days before a scheduling conference is held or a scheduling order is due under Rule 16(b), confer to consider the nature and basis of their claims and defenses and the possibilities for a prompt settlement or resolution of the case, to make or arrange for the disclosures required by Rule 26(a)(1), and to develop a proposed discovery plan that indicates the parties' views and proposals concerning:

(1) what changes should be made in the timing, form, or requirement for disclosures under Rule 26(a), including a statement as to when disclosures under Rule 26(a)(1) were made or will be made;

(2) the subjects on which discovery may be needed, when discovery should be completed, and whether discovery should be conducted in phases or be limited to or focused upon particular issues;

(3) what changes should be made in the limitations on discovery imposed under these rules or by local rule, and what other limitations should be imposed; and

(4) any other orders that should be entered by the court under Rule 26(c) or under Rule 16(b) and (c).

The attorneys of record and all unrepresented parties that have appeared in the case are jointly responsible for arranging the conference, for attempting in good faith to agree on the proposed discovery plan, and for submitting to the court within 14 days after the conference a written report outlining the plan. A court may order that the parties or attorneys attend the conference in person. If necessary to comply with its expedited schedule for Rule 16(b) conferences, a court may by local rule (i) require that the conference between the parties occur fewer than 21 days before the scheduling conference is held or a scheduling order is due under Rule 16(b), and (ii) require that the written report outlining the discovery plan be filed fewer than 14 days after the conference between the parties, or excuse the parties from submitting a written report and permit them to report orally on their discovery plan at the Rule 16(b) conference.

(g) Signing of Disclosures, Discovery Requests, Responses, and Objections.

    (1) Every disclosure made pursuant to subdivision (a)(1) or subdivision (a)(3) shall be signed by at least one attorney of record in the attorney's individual name, whose address shall be stated. An unrepresented party shall sign the disclosure and state the party's address. The signature of the attorney or party constitutes a certification that to the best of the signer's knowledge, information, and belief, formed after a reasonable inquiry, the disclosure is complete and correct as of the time it is made.

(2) Every discovery request, response, or objection made by a party represented by an attorney shall be signed by at least one attorney of record in the attorney's individual name, whose address shall be stated. An unrepresented party shall sign the request, response, or objection and state the party's address. The signature of the attorney or party constitutes a certification that to the best of the signer's knowledge, information, and belief, formed after a reasonable inquiry, the request, response, or objection is:

(A) consistent with these rules and warranted by existing law or a good faith argument for the extension, modification, or reversal of existing law;

(B) not interposed for any improper purpose, such as to harass or to cause unnecessary delay or needless increase in the cost of litigation; and

(C) not unreasonable or unduly burdensome or expensive, given the needs of the case, the discovery already had in the case, the amount in controversy, and the importance of the issues at stake in the litigation.

If a request, response, or objection is not signed, it shall be stricken unless it is signed promptly after the omission is called to the attention of the party making the request, response, or objection, and a party shall not be obligated to take any action with respect to it until it is signed.

(3) If without substantial justification a certification is made in violation of the rule, the court, upon motion or upon its own initiative, shall impose upon the person who made the certification, the party on whose behalf the disclosure, request, response, or objection is made, or both, an appropriate sanction, which may include an order to pay the amount of the reasonable expenses incurred because of the violation, including a reasonable attorney's fee.

Rule 37. Failure to Make Disclosure or Cooperate in Discovery: Sanctions

(a) **Motion for Order Compelling Disclosure or Discovery.** A party, upon reasonable notice to other parties and all persons affected thereby, may apply for an order compelling disclosure or discovery as follows:

(1) Appropriate Court. An application for an order to a party shall be made to the court in which the action is pending. An application for an order to a person who is not a party shall be made to the court in the district where the discovery is being, or is to be, taken.

(2) Motion.

(A) If a party fails to make a disclosure required by Rule 26(a), any other party may move to compel disclosure and for appropriate sanctions. The motion must include a certification that the movant has in good faith conferred or attempted to confer with the party not making the disclosure in an effort to secure the disclosure without court action.

(B) If a deponent fails to answer a question propounded or submitted under Rules 30 or 31, or a corporation or other entity fails to make a designation under Rule 30(b)(6) or 31(a), or a party fails to answer an interrogatory submitted under Rule 33, or if a party, in response to a request for inspection submitted under Rule 34, fails to respond that inspection will be permitted as requested or fails to permit inspection as requested, the discovering party may move for an order compelling an answer, or a designation, or an order compelling inspection in accordance with the request. The motion must include a certification that the movant has in good faith conferred or attempted to confer with the person or party failing to make the discovery in an effort to secure the information or material without court action. When taking a deposition on oral examination, the proponent of the question may complete or adjourn the examination before applying for an order.

(3) Evasive or Incomplete Disclosure, Answer, or Response. For purposes of this subdivision an evasive or incomplete disclosure, answer, or response is to be treated as a failure to disclose, answer, or respond.

(4) Expenses and Sanctions.

(A) If the motion is granted or if the disclosure or requested discovery is provided after the motion was filed, the court shall, after affording an opportunity to be heard, require the party or deponent whose conduct necessitated the motion or the party or attorney advising such conduct or both of them to pay to the moving party the reasonable expenses incurred in making the motion, including attorney's fees, unless the court finds that the motion was filed without the movant's first making a good faith effort to obtain the disclosure of discovery without court action, or that the opposing party's nondisclosure, response, or objection was substantially justified, or that other circumstances make an award of expenses unjust.

(B) If the motion is denied, the court may enter any protective order authorized under Rule 26(c) and shall, after affording an opportunity to be heard, require the moving party or the attorney filing the motion or both of them to pay to the party or deponent who opposed the motion the reasonable expenses incurred in opposing the motion, including attorney's fees, unless the court finds that the making of the motion was substantially justified or that other circumstances make an award of expenses unjust.

(C) If the motion is granted in part and denied in part, the court may enter any protective order authorized under

Rule 26(c) and may, after affording an opportunity to be heard, apportion the reasonable expenses incurred in relation to the motion among the parties and persons in a just manner.

(b) Failure to Comply with Order.

(1) Sanctions by Court in District Where Deposition Is Taken. If a deponent fails to be sworn or to answer a question after being directed to do so by the court in the district in which the deposition is being taken, the failure may be considered a contempt of that court.

(2) Sanctions by Court in Which Action Is Pending. If a party or an officer, director, or managing agent of a party or a person designated under Rule 30(b)(6) or 31(a) to testify on behalf of a party fails to obey an order to provide or permit discovery, including an order made under subdivision (a) of this rule or Rule 35, or if a party fails to obey an order entered under Rule 26(f), the court in which the action is pending may make such orders in regard to the failure as are just, and among others the following:

(A) An order that the matters regarding which the order was made or any other designated facts shall be taken to be established for the purposes of the action in accordance with the claim of the party obtaining the order;

(B) An order refusing to allow the disobedient party to support or oppose designated claims or defenses, or prohibiting that party from introducing designated matters in evidence;

(C) An order striking out pleadings or parts thereof, or staying further proceedings until the order is obeyed, or dismissing the action or proceeding or any part thereof, or rendering a judgment by default against the disobedient party;

(D) In lieu of any of the foregoing orders or in addition thereto, an order treating as a contempt of court the failure to obey any orders except an order to submit to a physical or mental examination;

(E) Where a party has failed to comply with an order under Rule 35(a) requiring that party to produce another for examination, such orders as are listed in paragraphs (A), (B), and (C) of this subdivision, unless the party failing to comply shows that that party is unable to produce such person for examination.

In lieu of any of the foregoing orders or in addition thereto, the court shall require the party failing to obey the order or the attorney advising that party or both to pay the reasonable expenses, including attorney's fees, caused by the failure, unless the court finds that the failure was substantially justified or that other circumstances make an award of expenses unjust.

(c) Failure to Disclose; False or Misleading Disclosure; Refusal to Admit.

(1) A party that without substantial justification fails to disclose information required by Rule 26(a) or 26(e)(1), or to amend a prior response to discovery as required by Rule 26(e)(2), is not, unless such failure is harmless, permitted to use as evidence at a trial, at a hearing, or on a motion any witness or information not so disclosed. In addition to or in lieu of this sanction, the court, on motion and after affording an opportunity to be heard, may impose other appropriate sanctions. In addition to requiring payment of reasonable expenses, including attorney's fees, caused by the failure, these sanctions may include any of the actions authorized under Rule 37(b)(2)(A), (B), and (C) and may include informing the jury of the failure to make the disclosure.

(2) If a party fails to admit the genuineness of any document or the truth of any matter as requested under Rule 36, and if the party requesting the admissions thereafter proves the genuineness of the document or the truth of the matter, the requesting party may apply to the court for an order requiring the other party to pay the reasonable expenses incurred in making that proof, including reasonable attorney's fees. The court shall make the order unless it finds that (A) the request was held objectionable pursuant to Rule 36(a), or (B) the admission sought was of no substantial importance, or (C) the party failing to admit had reasonable ground to believe that the party might prevail on the matter, or (D) there was other good reason for the failure to admit.

(d) Failure of Party to Attend at Own Deposition or Serve Answers to Interrogatories or Respond to Request for Inspection. If a party or an officer, director, or managing agent of a party or a person designated under Rule 30(b)(6) or 31(a) to testify on behalf of a party fails (1) to appear before the officer who is to take the deposition, after being served with a proper notice, or (2) to serve answers or objections to interrogatories submitted under Rule 33, after proper service of the interrogatories, or (3) to serve a written response to a request for inspection submitted under Rule 34, after proper service of the request, the court in which the action is pending on motion may make such orders in regard to the failure as are just, and among others it may take any action authorized under subparagraphs (A), (B), and (C) of subdivision (b)(2) of this rule. Any motion specifying a failure under clause (2) or (3) of this subdivision shall include a certification that the movant has in good faith conferred or attempted to confer with the party failing to answer or respond in an effort to obtain such answer or response without court action. In lieu of any order or in addition thereto, the court shall require the party failing to act or the attorney advising that party or both to pay the reasonable expenses, including attorney's fees, caused by the failure unless the court finds that the failure was substantially justified or that other circumstances make an award of expenses unjust.

The failure to act described in this subdivision may not be excused on the ground that the discovery sought is objectionable unless the party failing to act has a pending motion for a protective order as provided by Rule 26(c).

(e) [Abrogated]

(f) [Repealed. Pub.L 96-481, Title II, § 205(a), Oct. 21. 1980, 94 Stat. 2330.]

(g) Failure to Participate in the Framing of a Discovery Plan. If a party or a party's attorney fails to participate in good faith in the development and submission of a proposed discovery plan as required by Rule 26(f), the court may, after opportunity for hearing, require such party or attorney to pay to any other party the reasonable expenses, including attorney's fees, caused by the failure.

Index

Expert Rules